Selling Yourself to Employers

 THE ESSENTIAL JOB-HUNTING GUIDE

Tom and Gaynor O'Neil

NEW
HOLLAND

First published in 2011 by New Holland Publishers (NZ) Ltd
Auckland • Sydney • London • Cape Town

www.newhollandpublishers.co.nz

218 Lake Road, Northcote, Auckland 0627, New Zealand
Unit 1, 66 Gibbes Street, Chatswood, NSW 2067, Australia
86–88 Edgware Road, London W2 2EA, United Kingdom
80 McKenzie Street, Cape Town 8001, South Africa

ISBN: 978 1 86966 326 1

Publishing manager: Christine Thomson
Editor: Clare McIntosh
Design: IslandBridge
Cover design: Nick Turzynski
Author photograph: Cary Johnson

National Library of New Zealand Cataloguing-in-Publication Data

O'Neil, Tom.
Selling yourself to employers : the essential job-hunting guide
/ Tom O'Neil, Gaynor O'Neil ; editor, Clare McIntosh.
ISBN 978-1-86966-326-1
1. Job hunting. 2. Employment interviewing. I. O'Neil, Gaynor.
ll. McIntosh, Clare. Ill. Title.
650.14—dc 22

1 3 5 7 9 10 8 6 4 2

Colour reproduction by Image Print, Auckland
Printed in China at Everbest Printing Co, on paper sourced from
sustainable forests.

Contents

Introduction

In the business of recruitment and human resources, we continually come into contact with candidates who have a good deal of potential. However, they are unable to demonstrate to us how they have added measurable value in their positions with previous and current employers, thereby failing to convince us (or others) to interview or recruit them.

The problem is that most people have no idea how to actually 'sell' themselves effectively to potential employers. They don't realise that in the job hunt they become a product, which must highlight, in a tangible fashion, the best features and achievements in a way that ensures potential purchasers (résumé screeners and interviewers) will take notice.

The aim of this book is to help you understand the ways to increase your chances of gaining a dream job, through more effective selling of yourself with your résumé, during interviews and through networking.

When you sell yourself professionally, recruiters and employers take you more seriously, and this will result in more job opportunities and higher-value job offers.

Gaynor and I have over sixty years of experience in the human resources and recruitment industries, and between us we have interviewed approximately 30,000 people and have screened more than 180,000 résumés.

With sections on résumés, cover letters, interviewing tips, networking, direct marketing, salary negotiation and career goal setting, *Selling Yourself to Employers* is the essential job-hunting career guide.

Tom and Gaynor O'Neil

Authors' note

We use the word résumé as a generic term for curriculum vitae or CV. While a résumé usually means a shorter-form document in Canada and the United States, in most markets the three terms are used interchangeably, so when an employer asks for a résumé they are effectively asking for a CV, and vice versa.

All web resources and sites were checked prior to printing. We can take no responsibility in cases where websites have changed or resources are no longer available.

Section I

Selling yourself to employers

What the job-hunting process is all about

You are a product that must be sold effectively. The fact that the department dealing with staff is called the Human Resources Department states it all:

You are a RESOURCE.

Because you are a resource, you must sell yourself.

Think of yourself as a product. What makes this product stand out from its competitors? What is this product's unique selling points? What makes it better than the other products?

As a former recruiter and human resources management consultant for Deloittes, I am continually in contact with candidates, who have significant potential, vying for positions. However, many cannot demonstrate how they have added value to previous or current employers, and this means they fail to convince me that they should be interviewed or recruited.

The problem is that most people have no idea how to actually 'sell and market' themselves effectively to potential employers. They do not realise that when job-hunting they become a 'product'. And because of this they must tangibly highlight their best 'features and benefits' to ensure the potential purchasers (résumé screeners and interviewers) take notice of them.

For example, imagine if the world's number one golfer presented their résumé like this:

Occupation	Golfer
Responsibilities	Hit ball
	Hit ball again
	Tap ball lightly
	Tap ball into hole

Would this sell them as the world's number one golfer? Certainly not.

Another example could be selling an expensive Ferrari. You do not put an advertisement in the Cars For Sale section of your local newspaper with the text:

> Car, 4 wheels, engine. Goes. $100,000.

It is important that you 'sell' the features and benefits of the car to maximise interest in it (and to justify its price). Therefore, the advertisement should read something like this:

> Ferrari 360. 2006, low miles. 560 horsepower, top speed
> of 300 kph. Racing red. Only $100,000. Live the dream.

When looking for a job, you must remember you are about to sell one of the most important products you can ever imagine. That product is YOU. From the start, you must have the same mindset about selling yourself as you would selling an internationally renowned product or service.

So, we have established that you are the product when job-hunting. Now you must see yourself as an expert salesperson, selling this wonderful product.

You must know what you can offer an employer and what sets you apart from the competition. *Remember: If you only say what you get paid to do, you are only as good as everyone else.*

The fundamentals of employment are changing massively

The job world has undergone a radical transformation over the last 50 years. Gone are 'jobs for life' and with it the security that brings. A funny example of this is when I was completing a redundancy support course for a range of government employees, some of whom had been with the same company for 40-plus years. One older manager told the group that he originally wanted to be a land surveyor. As a young job-hunter he diligently went to the government offices, where he was told to register his interest on the fifth floor. He got off, by mistake, on the third floor, and spent the next 20 years as an accountant, only breaking into land surveying after half a career life had passed.

With the advent of the internet, contracting, job-sharing, and working from home, the United States Bureau of Labor predicts that the average young person in the United States will have about nine jobs between the ages of 18 and 32. That's one job every 18 to 19 months. Craig Rispin, a business futurologist, goes as far as to say that all jobs will be freelance in the future.

When I started working in recruitment 20 years ago, being in a job for five years was thought to be about the right amount of time. Today, that same period of time says to a potential employer that you have got stale and are afraid of challenge.

VERY IMPORTANT – Do not let this worry you, however, if you are working in a role you enjoy for an employer you really like. Do not jump ship just because you think it is the right thing to do for your career.

Employers are not interested in you

Remember that an employer is not initially interested in you as an individual. An employer is only interested in getting the right person for the job.

When a company advertises a vacant position, they are not giving away $48,000 to a customer services consultant for the fun of it. They have to be judicious with the money that they have at their disposal, and able to fully account to the company owners or shareholders for every dollar they spend on employing someone.

On most occasions, a company advertises a vacancy for one of two reasons:

- The company has grown, has gained more clients or sold more services and there is now more work to be done.
- An employee has left the company and they must be replaced.

If a position is not filled quickly, the other members of the team will have to do the job of the person who has left. This will cause extreme frustration over the short-to-medium term, and lead to others leaving the company as they begin to feel overworked.

The vacancy becomes a 'problem' for the company, so the employer is seeking a 'solution'. It is vital that you tailor your entire recruitment approach as a solution specifically to the employer you are applying to. This means tweaking or tailoring your résumé and cover letter as well as paying particular attention to the key points employers and recruiters are highlighting in their advertisement.

Job advertisements

Generally speaking, recruitment advertisements take the following form:

- Job title
- What your key responsibilities are in this role
- What the company seeks in a candidate

For example:

Customer Service Centre Supervisor

We are excited to start the search for a special person to lead our busy Customer Service Centre. The successful applicant will have previous experience and proven success in a customer service position as well as excellent computer skills, the ability to thrive in a fast-paced environment and to lead from the front.

Duties and responsibilities will include:

- Supervising the customer service team of 4–5 staff
- Training and staff recruitment when necessary
- Reviewing and maintaining customer service records and forms
- Order entry processing
- Managing the daily workflow
- Resolution of customer complaints

We are looking for a great 'multitasker', someone who can build a rapport with customers/clients and has a 'can-do' attitude. You must also have proven leadership and coaching skills as well as excellent verbal and written communication skills.

The key here is to look at the final paragraph. There you find all the key skills, attributes and experience they are seeking. In this example the key 'solutions' for the employer include:

- Strong multitasking ability
- Excellent relationship development skills
- Proactive and 'can-do' attitude to work
- Demonstrated leadership and coaching background
- Very good written and oral communication and interpersonal skills.

It is important to 'mirror' these attributes in your résumé, cover letter and all your interviews to maximise your opportunity of being seen as the best solution to their problem – ahead of all other competing candidates. To be seen not as just another person sending in a résumé and hoping for the best.

Remember – the job hunt is a race. But unlike the Olympics, there is no prize for coming second. Only disappointment and wasted time. Therefore, work hard on becoming the employer's solution, and you will gain your next role in record time.

The magic word is 'Result'

At the end of the day, the job-hunting process is a race. Your job is to come first! Most résumés list a host of general responsibilities one does during one's career; however, what really gets an employer excited is the 'results' that came from those responsibilities. Demonstrating 'results' you achieved throughout your career makes the decision to recruit you easier, because it gives the employer what they want to see and highlights what sets you apart from all the others trying to get that role!

Avoid cluttering the résumé with unnecessary personal opinions and unsubstantiated comments such as 'hardworking', 'honest' and 'creative'. Employers want evidence of your performance record and you will get the chance to highlight these 'results' in the Major Achievement sections of your résumé.

Other comments to avoid include such things as:

- 'Significantly increased database of clients.'
- 'Visited eight potential clients per day.'
- 'Sent direct mail to 10,000 possible new clients.'

These statements are not what the employer needs to read – they do not describe quantifiable results.

To make the three statements above more useful and better suited to the purpose of attracting the attention of a potential employer, you could expand them as follows:

- 'Increased database of clients from 150 to 300. Result: doubling turnover in the territory over a two-year period.'

- 'Visited eight potential clients per day. Ratio of sales produced to sales calls made was one in four. The average sale was $2000 and consistently averaged two sales per day, or $20,000 per week. Result: after three months, sales increased by 50% over the previous incumbent's performance.'

- 'Sent direct mail to 10,000 prospective clients. Result: this promotion converted into 360 sales for a total of $2.6 million.'

This gets the reader's attention and makes you more attractive as a prospective employee.

Discovering your achievements and how to effectively 'sell' yourself to employers

The O'Neil Major Achievements Questionnaire (OMAQ) helps individuals to discover their key career and personal achievements. It is published in the 2008–2011 editions of the world's best-selling career guide *What Color Is Your Parachute?*

The OMAQ tool helps you to discover both your career and personal achievements, giving you tangible examples you can highlight in both your résumé and at the interview.

It is vital you know not just who you are, but also how to market yourself in a way an employer can easily understand.

The easiest and best possible way is to define your achievements in a quantifiable and ordered way, demonstrating what you have achieved in the past. This, in turn, will show what you are capable of in the future.

O'Neil Major Achievements Questionnaire

The O'Neil Major Achievements Questionnaire helps candidates methodically discover areas of achievement (results) in their career and personal life, which they can include in their résumé as well as draw out in interviews. This questionnaire takes time to complete (from 30 minutes to two hours), but the answers could well mean the difference between your getting or not getting that next job offer.

The strength of the O'Neil Major Achievements Questionnaire is that it has been quoted in the world's number one selling career guide *What Color Is Your Parachute?* every year since 2008.

Think of your working and personal experiences and the skills you believe you have learnt. Which ones are you proud of? What things have you done in your career that few other people have achieved? In your résumé, assign these achievements to both the company and the position in which you worked.

It is important to be quantitative when you do this – for example, mention specific dates, percentages, dollar values, brand names, etc. But remember that it might not be appropriate to reveal potentially confidential information to prospective employers. A good question you could ask yourself is: 'Is this information common knowledge within the industry or is it commercially sensitive?'

Key questions to ask yourself

Education

- Did you win any awards for study or gain any scholarships?
- Did you have any high (A- or above) individual or overall grades? If so, what were the papers and grades?
- Were you involved in any committees, etc.?
- If you are a recent graduate, detail the courses you have completed for your qualification.

- Did you work while you were studying? If so, did you receive any promotions or gain any achievements in the role?

Sales / Account management

- Have you consistently exceeded your set budget in a role? If so, by what percentage or dollar value?

- Have you exceeded your set budget in a particular month(s)/quarter(s)? If so, by what percentage or by what dollar value?

- What level are you compared to in regard to the other sales professionals in your company? (For example, number 3 out of 20 in the sales team.)

- Have you increased market share? If so, by what percentage or dollar value?

- Have you brought on/gained any major clients?

- What major clients are/were you responsible for managing and selling to?

- Have you managed to generate repeat business/increased current business? If so, by what percentage or dollar value?

- Have you won any internal/external sales awards?

- Did you develop any new successful promotional/marketing ideas that increased sales?

Administration / Customer services / Accounts

- Did you set up or improve any systems and/or processes?

- Did you take any old administration or paperwork-based systems and convert them to an IT-based system?

- Was there a quantifiable difference in the company/business unit when you first joined the business/project and when you completed the project/left the business?

- Did you assist in reducing customer complaints, etc.?

Event / Logistical management

- Have you managed any major suppliers?

- Have you been involved in any major relocation projects?

- Have you organised any events/conferences? If so, how large were they (both people attending and total budget if possible) and where and when were the event(s) held?

General

- Did you have any performance targets you had to achieve? Did you consistently meet these or exceed them?

- Were you promoted? If so, in what years and to which roles?

- How long have you spent within an industry? For example, 12 years' experience in the fashion industry.

- Extra authority awarded after a period of time within a role? (For example, commenced as receptionist, after three months, awarded with further clerical responsibilities including data entry and accounts payable.) Note that commonly these responsibilities awarded to you do not affect your job title and/or salary.

- Were you involved in any special projects outside your job description? What was the result?

- Have you been asked to take part in any trainee management courses/management development programmes?

- Have you dealt with any overseas branches, operations, suppliers or customers?

Positive feedback

- Did you receive any business awards? (For example, acknowledged for support/service of clients/staff, etc.)

- Did you receive any written or verbal client/customer/ managerial commendations/ letters of praise?

- Can you think of any occasions where you gave excellent customer service and how did you know the customer was satisfied? (What was the outcome? How did it benefit the company?)

Responsibility

- Were you responsible for the purchase of any goods/services in your business? (For example, air travel/PC acquisition.)

- Have you had any budget responsibility? If so, to what level? (For example, responsibility for divisional budget of $200,000 per annum.)

- Have you had any staff responsibility? If so, to what capacity/how many staff were you responsible for?

- Were you responsible for any official or unofficial training? If so, what type, for whom, and how many people have you trained? (For example, responsible for training 12 new staff members in all customer services aspects, as well as in the in-house computer system.)

- Were you responsible for any official or unofficial coaching/mentoring of staff?

- Have you been responsible for any aspects of recruitment? (For example, writing the advertising, screening, interviewing, verbal reference checks, etc.?)

Memberships

- Do you hold memberships to any industry bodies?

- Have you been a representative on any committees? (For example, a health and safety committee.)

- Do you belong or have you belonged to any professional clubs such as Toastmasters, Lions or Rotary?

Mechanical / Print / Technical

- What machine and/or systems experience have you gained?
- Are there any special truck/car/machine brands that you have serviced, maintained or repaired?
- Have you commissioned or set up any machinery at work?

Voluntary / Community / Unpaid work

- Have you completed voluntary or unpaid work for any organisation or company? (For example, a church, school, community service, special needs organisation.)

Building / Construction / Electrical / Plumbing

- What major projects have you worked on? How much did the project cost? (For example, reception refurbishment – ABC Bank (Head Office) $1.2 million.)

IT / IS / Computer / PC

- What systems/software and hardware experience do you have?
- What IT brands have you serviced, maintained or repaired? What software have you utilised?
- Have you developed any websites or systems software? If so, what were they, and did they positively affect the business? What was the successful outcome?
- Were you involved in any special projects outside your job description?

Published / Presented Work

- Have you had articles, papers or features published in any magazines, journals or books? If so, what publications and when?

- Have you presented any topics at any conferences or completed any public speaking? If so, what subjects have you talked about and how large was the audience?

To assist in drawing out your achievements

If you are having trouble working out your achievements, complete this task below for each role, starting with your current position and working backwards.

S – Skills (What skills did you learn in this role?)

E – Experiences (What experiences did you have?)

A – Achievements (What achievements did you gain?)

L – Link the relevant aspects to the job you are applying for.

Remember to use a strong achievements focus when you imagine your future employment. Think about how you can add value in the future. For example:

- Get involved with special projects outside your main job
- See how you can improve systems
- Help with training new staff in PC systems you know well
- Keep track of your commendations.

Actively hunt out new opportunities to complete achievements that can then be used effectively when you apply for future roles.

Moving forward into employment

The information you generate asking the above questions will also be handy during performance appraisal time because it will allow you to demonstrate in a quantitative way what you have achieved in your role. This could well assist in improving your overall performance rating and increasing your annual bonus and / or salary.

Section II

Developing your résumé and cover letter

Getting your brochure or résumé right

Your résumé is your brochure to the employing world. As specialist résumé writers, we have seen many amazing examples of poor spelling, crazy details and general written incompetence from all sorts of job-seekers. Examples of what not to do include:

- No name, telephone or email contact details. This generates a problem if you want to call the person in for an interview.

- Quote from a résumé: 'The meek and the mild will be the rungs to the ladder of my success.'

- Company – ABC Consulting. Position – Analist.

- A person spelt their first name wrong at the start of their résumé in type sized point 22.

- Quote from a résumé: 'Some time we need to go to the customer's <u>horse</u> to help them set up they computer and network.'

- On one occasion, an HR professional who should have known better sent us a 39-page résumé. This résumé had 10,700 words (that's about 40% of the words in this book . . .).

- Our personal favourite: 'I am a stickler for detail as in any contract environment the devil is in the details and a good project manager must appreciate the need to <u>ot the I's</u> and cross the T's.'

Companies spend millions of dollars creating professional brochures to market their products to their target audiences. Your résumé is your brochure – it must 'sell you' to employers just as a travel brochure sells travel to an exciting location. It must highlight the key points that meet the employer's requirements. In addition to this, it must be brief – i.e. have enough information to sell you within two to four pages.

Different sections of a résumé and their purpose

A successful résumé would always include most of the sections detailed below. The following order is also important because you are trying to guide the reader on a journey. First, you must highlight yourself as being a 'solution' to the reader, then demonstrate the results and achievements you have gained throughout your career, reinforcing the fact that *you are the one* they should be interviewing.

Objective

The Objective has been described as the 'soul of the résumé' and appears immediately after your name and contact details. It instantly informs the assessor on what you require in a work role. If this is done well, it will give the impression that you are a focused person who knows what they want in life. This is always a good look.

The Objective is an important statement in gaining the attention of the employer. Put as simply as possible, the aim is to show what you want and what skills you have to help you get what you want. This makes it easier for the employer to decide if you meet the needs of the company.

The Objective needs to be brief and to the point. For example:

• The role that you are seeking.

- The key skills/qualifications that you can bring to the position.

If you can tailor your résumé directly to the role, your potential employer will see at a glance whether you are someone they can use or just 'another résumé'.

Sadly, a significant percentage of résumés received are discarded because the employer cannot easily identify the applicant's requirements. Tailoring a résumé makes the reader's job easier. If you can do this, you have a much higher chance of progressing to the interview stage.

If you tailor a résumé to a company name or industry (which we suggest), always be careful that you change the Objective when you apply for another position. Human resources managers always grimace when they see a résumé that has an objective for another company on the résumé. You do not want to pitch your résumé at a possible competitor.

Good examples include:

OBJECTIVE

Seeking the role of sales representative with ABC Realty, where a successful business development and account management background within the real estate industry can be utilised.

Seeking the role of quantity surveyor with ABC Company, where strong estimating and quoting experience within the construction and building sectors can be utilised.

Remember when writing your Objective to always have the employer's needs in mind.

Personal Summary

The Summary is effectively the front porch of the career house. If it is not well presented then no one will want to enter. The employer could make incorrect negative judgments or, even worse, stop reading your résumé altogether if the first paragraph is not right.

The Summary is just that – a summary. It should be easy to read at a glance, contain the highlights, and pique the employer's curiosity and desire to know more about you.

To make certain the employer quickly feels you are on the same wavelength as themselves, highlight the required skills they detail in their advertisement and match yours accordingly. Ensure these are incorporated into the summary to make sure you stand out among the other candidates.

Use short sentences/statement paragraphs and bullet points. Allow space around your bullet points to ensure that they stand out. For example:

Personal Summary:

- Office management professional, degree educated, with strong experience within the customer services and administrative environments.

- Results driven, with a business-minded approach to office management, which resulted in rapid promotion within current company.

- Acting as a role model and leading by example led to acquiring mentoring and training of staff to create a cohesive and dynamic working environment, shortly after joining present company.

- Excellent communication and interpersonal skills with the ability to relate effectively and professionally to people at all levels in a company.

- Acknowledged by management for high attention to detail and ability to manage numerous projects simultaneously.

- Proactive and positive team member, with a 'can-do' attitude to all projects.

- Recognised for operating effectively in fast-paced and pressured environments.

- Quick to learn new principles and concepts, with a strong focus towards ongoing learning and personal development.

Personal Attributes / Quotes

Take quotes from previous employers, customer references, commendations, appraisals, etc. and include these in the résumé. For example:

PERSONAL ATTRIBUTES

I found Peter's biggest strength is his ability to create, implement and monitor processes … He also displayed a determination to succeed and was able to build an excellent rapport with the rest of our team members and stakeholders … Peter has always shown himself to be completely trustworthy, reliable and an extremely hard worker … He is respected by myself and all who know him and is of complete integrity and honesty.

Lisa Abbey, Operations Team Leader – Microsoft Corporation, New York

---

Using personal quotes is a very effective way to demonstrate 'soft' competencies (i.e. team player / great communicator) in a tangible way. This is also how you gain 'instant credibility' and give the recipient confidence to proceed.

Career History

An employer's interest in your career history is generally as follows:

Period	Employer's interest	Key responsibilities
Last 5 years	Very interested	6–8 bullet points
5–10 years	Quite interested	4–8 bullet points
10–15 years	Slightly interested	2–4 bullet points
15–20 years	Somewhat interested	1–2 bullet points
20+ years	Not interested	General statement

You should therefore devote relative detail in relation to these periods. So, the more interested in a period the employer is, the more you want to inform them of your responsibilities by providing greater detail. You also want to make the section brief and easy to read, so present the information in clear bullet points.

Remember, the employer is more interested in your *latest* role. The positions you held when you had just left school are the least important. This is why your career history is sequenced with the latest or current roles coming first then working backwards to least recent.

If you are uncertain about how to describe your responsibilities, visit a recruitment website or job board and identify a position that is similar to your role. Using this as a template, describe your duties clearly. For example:

**2003–Current   LAND MANAGEMENT LIMITED
PROJECT LEADER**

Key responsibilities:

- Define project scope, goals and deliverables that support business goals in collaboration with senior management and stakeholders.

- Effectively communicate and manage various project management timelines, processes and methodologies with customers and internal staff.

- Coordinate project plans for cross-functional teams.

- Develop project plans and status reports as well as comprehensive commercial documentation.

- Serve as the key contact and communications point for the projects.

- Estimate the resources and participants needed to achieve project goals.

- Identify and manage project dependencies and critical paths.

- Track and report project tasks, activity, documentation, and time tracking.

Major achievements

Under each position (not company because you may have been pro-moted within one company), highlight your major achievements to demonstrate the success you have had in this position. For example:

Major achievements:

- Successfully exceeded all 'work unit per day' targets. On occasion, exceeded targets by up to 45%.

- Using strict project management methodologies, successfully led the delivery of key projects on time and within budget. Examples include:
  – Managed a $1 million project to assess, design and deliver a solution for customers in remote areas of Montana, USA.
  – Developed and implemented a new delivery system that reduced overall logistics costs by 12%.

- Developed and implemented a number of effective systems to streamline administrative and IT operations within the department. Examples include:
  - Set up a new IT system (APD Pro) to successfully monitor new work practices, both internally and onsite.
- Received numerous customer and managerial commendations for providing a consistently high standard of surveying support and service.
- Awarded further responsibility for training new and current staff in survey process procedures as well as internal systems.

Qualifications and Professional Development

Key qualifications should be included in your résumé. These include degrees and diplomas.

Standard courses should also be included, if they are relevant. However, obscure courses or courses that may not have much appeal to an employer should be left out.

For example, if you are applying for the role of Office Administrator, you would include the relevant qualifications and courses you completed. For example:

- Bachelor of Business Administration – Texas State University (2008)
- Microsoft Word Certificate – Texas Institute of Learning (2008)
- Time Management for Administrators – ABC Training (2007)
- Customer Service Fundamentals – Andrews Training Centre (2005)

Computer Knowledge

Unless you are an IT specialist, only highlight the key software programs you can use. If you are an IT specialist, you would look to include this after the Personal Summary section at the start of the résumé to draw strong attention to these skills and knowledge. If you are not an IT professional, this section tends to sit after the Qualifications and Professional Development section.

For example:

- Experienced in using Microsoft Windows, Word, Excel, PowerPoint, Adobe Acrobat and OpenOffice as well as a variety of in-house software packages.

Personal

Including personal details in your CV gives the employer information about yourself. However, it is important to include only details that can be perceived as positive. What's acceptable to include in this section has changed considerably over the years. In fact, this is the section most employers will not ask you about as they fear breaking Equal Employment Opportunity law.

Feel free to include, or not include, any the following. Only include details on these if you think it favours your chances of gaining an interview:

- Marital status
- Health
- Non-smoker

Voluntary Work

This section tends to be left off general résumés. However, it can give insight into a person's community spirit as well as demonstrate responsibility and personal development outside of the work realm. This section is focused on actual voluntary experience you have completed. For example:

Voluntary work:

- Involved in a number of community support programmes including:
    - Collector for various animal welfare appeals (2009–)
    - Member School Board of Trustees (2004–2011)
    - Church Board Member (2007–2010)

Published Work / Presentations

Highlighting any published work or presentations you may have made at conferences can reinforce your standing as a specialist in these key areas.

Interests

Although this may seem irrelevant to your professional life, your interests and hobbies can say a lot about you as a person. For example, team sports indicate a team player in the workplace. Someone who enjoys reading may have keen intellectual interests. Try to ensure that you come across as a healthy, well-rounded person, without bending the truth.

Verbal Referees

Ensure that your verbal referees know potential employers are going to contact them about your suitability for employment. It is always embarrassing if this does not happen and the referee is taken by surprise. Let your referees know when you start your job hunt and be sure to gain their approval prior to them being contacted. This will give your referees an opportunity to more accurately remember you and your performance before they are contacted, which could result in making their reference very positive.

You generally need two to three professional referees, and these should not include relatives or friends.

Having referees in your résumé can speed up the interview process. For example, if an employer is very keen to employ you and can complete the verbal references in one day, a job offer could hopefully follow next. If they don't have contact details, they now need to contact you and get your authorisation to contact your verbal referees. If you are unavailable, this means other potential candidates can enter the scene in the meantime and become real contenders for your job.

Referees also add credibility to your approach. Include your referees' names, positions, companies and contact details, which may include a mobile number, a land line and an email address.

What NOT to put into your résumé

Always remember that a résumé is your brochure. It is therefore crucial that you have a long hard think about what you do and do not include. Ask yourself these questions:

- Is the information positive and in line with what the employer is looking for in a future employee?
- Does it show the benefits of an employer hiring me?
- If required, does it show that I am either a 'profit opportunity' or a 'cost benefit' to the company?

A résumé is not a disclaimer

While you must not lie in your résumé , you want to ensure that you are shown in a favourable light. (See 'Damage control', p. 122.)

Check out www.tomoneil.com/templates.html for a free MS Word résumé template.

Sample résumés

Assistant Accountant

John is an Assistant Accountant with five years' experience in the business software and real estate industries, in a variety of accounts roles. Through hard work, he was awarded further IT and finance responsibilities in his current position, and has a solid knowledge of a wide range of accounting legislation and systems.

John Smith

159 Hope Drive, New Windsor 90234
Mobile: (0274) 555 1827   Email: jsmith777@email.com

OBJECTIVE

Seeking the role of Assistant Accountant with ABC Business Services, where strong financial and business administration qualifications and experience can be utilised.

PERSONAL SUMMARY

- Proven experience with accounting legislation and systems, including taxation, auditing, fixed assets, accounts payable/receivable and financial accounting.

- Willing to learn new accounting and financial principles, with a genuine focus towards ongoing professional development. Passion to become CA qualified in the future.

- Solid background using a wide range of systems including MYOB, Quicken, MS Excel, SQL Server, MS Access, Customer Relationship Manager (CRM) and MS Outlook. Excellent keyboard skills.

- Excellent communication and interpersonal skills, with the ability to develop strong relationships at all staff levels.

- Qualifications include a Bachelor of Business (majoring in Accounting & Commercial Law) – New York State University.

PERSONAL ATTRIBUTES

John launched into his role with enthusiasm and professionalism that had both myself and my partner impressed. John has contributed new ideas and improvements to our practice, as well as introducing new clients to the business.

Brian Andrews, CEO – Innovative Business Systems

CAREER HISTORY

Jan 2009–Present   Innovative Business Software

- **Commenced** as an Accountants Assistant.
- **Due to a professional and quality-first approach**, awarded with further senior-level financial and IT management responsibilities.

Key responsibilities:

- Oversee financial and accounts management for the business.
- Manage accounts payable/receivable and follow up debtors and credit control.
- Complete invoicing and reporting.
- Professionally handle debtor queries.

Major achievements:

- Developed and implemented a number of effective systems to streamline administrative operations within the business.
- Provided key input into the development of a major accounting system implementation for ABC Ltd. Identified the internal control weakness in the current system and recommended changes.
- Received numerous customer and managerial commendations for providing a consistently high standard of support and service.

Mar 2006–Dec 2008   *Systemz Real Estate Ltd*
Accountants Clerk

Key responsibilities:

- Complete general book-keeping and accounts using MYOB.

- Oversee invoicing and debtors reconciliation.

- Manage credit control and debt collections for the business.

- Organise and coordinate sales budgets.

- Liaise directly with clients regarding finance terms and accounts.

Major achievements:

- Demonstrated strong practical skills in prioritising, multitasking and time management as well as the ability to work autonomously.

QUALIFICATIONS AND PROFESSIONAL DEVELOPMENT

- Bachelor of Business (major in Accounting & Commercial Law) – New York State University (2009)

INTERESTS

- Interests include tennis, baseball, soccer, film and current events.

COMPUTER KNOWLEDGE

- Windows, MYOB, Quicken, SQL Server, MS Access, MS Word, Customer Relationship Manager (CRM) and MS Outlook.

REFEREES

- Brian Andrews, CEO – Innovative Business Systems
  Mob: (555) 123 6738

- Julie Wildon, General Manager – Systemz Real Estate Ltd
  Mob: (555) 123 8901   Email: julie.wildon@system.com

Sales Representative

Brian has worked in both the UK and Australia in the sales industry. He was promoted from Sales Administrator to Sales Representative in 2010 and has been very successful achieving and exceeding challenging sales targets in his current position.

Brian Kumar

2/22 Anderson Street, Oaktown 125 831
Mobile: (021) 555 5555   Email: kyr2@email.com

OBJECTIVE

Seeking the role of Sales Representative, where a strong background in business development and key account management can be utilised.

PERSONAL SUMMARY

- Business development professional with a proven background in successful sales. Focused on achieving set targets and business goals as well as delivering a high standard of customer service.

- Logical and analytical thinker, with a strong problem-solving approach to work. Displays initiative when seeking solutions and makes sound business decisions.

- Excellent communication, interpersonal and negotiation skills, with the ability to develop strong relationships and influence.

- Self-motivated and disciplined with a determined attitude to succeed.

PERSONAL ATTRIBUTES

Brian gained the team's trust very early on and was always ready to extend his help to all team members. Brian is also able to work on his own while meeting deadlines set out ahead of him and produced very good results. External relationships were also key to his role, which he managed with integrity at all times.

Ann Smithe, Sales Manager – ABC IT Systems

CAREER HISTORY

Jun 2006–Present   ABC IT Systems, Sydney, Australia

- **Commenced** as a Sales Administrator
- **In 2010, promoted** to the role of Sales Representative.

Key responsibilities:

- Build and maintain strong relationships with corporate clients and identify opportunities to increase service offerings.
- Identify potential clients and implement effective strategies to gain their business.
- Lead and facilitate business and sales presentations.
- Develop strong corporate networks within the local region.
- Proactively solve any issues directly or indirectly involving customers and the sales process.
- Ensure monthly targets are exceeded and the regular call cycle is maintained.

Major achievements:

- Successful at achieving and exceeding set key performance indicators (KPIs) and business development targets.
- Due to a professional and client-focused approach to work, developed a loyal client base as well as strong referral and repeat business.
- Awarded further responsibility for training new and current staff in quality-based customer services and sales techniques as well as internal systems.

Sep 2002–May 2006   Digital Audio London Ltd
Retail Sales Consultant

Key responsibilities:

- Meet monthly sales targets set by managers.
- Provide a consistently high standard of service to a diverse range of customers.
- Complete high-volume cash and credit handling.
- Sell high-technology products and solutions as well as develop strong relationships with both businesses and individual customers.
- Merchandise and display new stock effectively to drive further sales.

Major achievements:

- Recognised for performance excellence and superior customer service skills through feedback and surveys from customers.
- Successfully demonstrated the ability to work in team-based environments and to tight deadlines.
- Provided a high level of support and coaching to new team members.

QUALIFICATIONS AND PROFESSIONAL DEVELOPMENT

- National Diploma in Business – London University of Technology (2010)
- Advanced Sales for the IT Sector – Tom Hopkins Training (2009)
- Sales Success – Dale Carnegie Training (2009)

INTERESTS

- Interests include personal development, golf, cooking, theatre and socialising with family and friends.

COMPUTER KNOWLEDGE

- MS Windows, Mac OS, MS Word, MS Excel and MS Outlook.

REFEREES

- John Bridges, Sales Manager – ABC IT Systems
  Mob: (555) 777 1234

- Lisa Maxwell, General Manager – Digital Audio London Ltd
  Mob: (555) 888 1298

Junior Chef

Janelle graduated with a Diploma in Culinary Arts in 2010 and has a real passion for developing a strong career within hospitality. With four years' experience in the industry, she has been awarded further responsibility for training, mentoring and coaching other team members in the kitchen.

Janelle Anderson

188 Simpak Road, Eden Park, London N17 0AA
Telephone: (09) 570 5555   Mobile: (027) 888 5555
Email: JA1988@email.com

OBJECTIVE

Seeking role as sous chef where both qualifications and accomplishments in culinary arts, as well as special talent for food preparation, can be utilised.

PERSONAL SUMMARY

- Genuine passion for food, with a commitment to developing a strong career within this challenging and exciting industry.

- Excellent skills in food preparation and solid practical knowledge of:
    - Budgeting/planning
    - Stock management
    - Menu development
    - Kitchen hygiene
    - Health and safety
    - Food nutrition
    - Food technology
    - Cooking methods

- Strong communication and interpersonal skills with the ability to relate effectively and professionally to people at all levels.

- Proven ability to multitask, a high attention to detail and able to work to deadlines.
- Proactive and positive team member, with a 'can-do' attitude to all projects.

QUALIFICATIONS AND PROFESSIONAL DEVELOPMENT

- Diploma in Culinary Arts (Level 5) – New York University of Technology (2010)

  Papers:
  - Information Technology for Culinary Arts
  - Culinary Cooperative Education
  - Kitchen Management
  - Gastronomy
  - Advanced Culinary Practices and Principles I & II
  - Advanced Hot and Cold Desserts
  - Advanced Cakes and Pastry

- Workplace First Aid – ABC Safety Systems (2010)

CAREER HISTORY

2008–Current   Domus Café, Eden Park
Junior Chef

Key responsibilities:

- Train and mentor new kitchen staff.
- Prepare food using effective hygiene practices.
- Complete high-volume cash handling.
- Work flexible hours, within a team environment.
- Ensure compliance with company standards of product quality, service and cleanliness.

Major achievements:

- Received numerous customer and managerial commendations for providing a consistently high standard of support and service.

- Gained strong face-to-face customer services and communications experience as well as practical skills in prioritising, multitasking and time management.

- Awarded further responsibility for training staff in kitchen systems as well as customer services.

COMPUTER KNOWLEDGE

- General office-related products include MS Word, MS Excel, MS PowerPoint, Internet Explorer, MS Outlook as well as a variety of in-house software packages.

INTERESTS

- Interests include cooking, travel, tramping and reading.

REFEREES

- Bill Williams, Lecturer – London University of Technology
  Telephone: (555) 777 1234
  Email: billwilliams1965@email.com

- Haresh Singh, Manager/Owner – Domus Café
  Tel: (555) 545 7777
  Mob: (555) 888 777

Final word

Never be afraid to be creative in your approach to a future employer. We ran a career development course in Dunedin where one woman proceeded to tell me that her untraditional résumé was very successful. We quizzed her further and she then showed me what she had done. Frustrated at the low degree of interest her old résumé was generating, she drew two stick figures to represent herself and her husband and wrote some basic details about herself.

After photocopying 100 of these, she distributed them randomly to businesses within the city centre. Within a very short period of time a manager at a respected government department called her in and offered her a role immediately. He was taken by her desire to work hard as well as her creative and fun side, which was portrayed through her 'non-traditional' résumé.

Hello

We have just arrived in Dunedin to live.
Husband has a job – but I would like one too. My name is Joan and I am a mature woman with a great sense of humour. I have worked for various government departments, as well as Wellington Hospital, Lands and Deeds, Prison Service, GP Stationery and Wellington Polytechnic; all in admin roles, apart from the Prison Service. If you need a reliable, self-motivated person, please give me a call on

Thanks for your time.

The *Melbourne Age* reported on a college graduate seeking her first public relations role. She sent three firms a shoe in a box with a note saying, 'I'm just trying to get my foot in the door.' The cheesy technique worked because she stood out from the crowd of other applicants.

At the end of the day, what's really important is to strike a balance between creativity and professionalism. If you can do this effectively, you will be remembered for the right reasons and get an interview.

Cover letters – the frame to your résumé

Publishers around the world spend millions of dollars each year designing covers to promote and sell their books. A well-crafted dust jacket will entice the reader to delve further into the book, hopefully leading to enough excitement that they then make a purchase.

In the same way, a good cover letter should 'frame' the résumé, providing an enticing introduction to read further and learn more about the candidate it is representing.

It is not necessary to have a long cover letter. At a recent conference where we were speaking, an HR Manager, two recruitment consultants and a general manager were asked by the audience how long a cover letter should be. The resounding response from these professionals came as one immediate answer: 'ONE PAGE ONLY.'

A cover letter helps in the following ways:

- It shows the employer that you have researched their company.
- It demonstrates your ability to communicate professionally in a written format.
- It is usually your first point of contact, so it can set the tone for your whole relationship with the company.

Rules for cover letters

- Write a different cover letter for every prospective employer.
- Always write the letter to a particular person, ensuring the recipient's name is spelled correctly. If you do not know the name or the spelling, ring the company to find out.
- State why you are writing.

- Indicate the title of the position.
- Explain your reasons for interest in the organisation.
- Express your enthusiasm for the role.
- Communicate your motivation and strengths.
- Indicate how the employer can contact you.
- Check spelling and grammar.

Cover letter structure

The basic structure of a cover letter includes four sections. Avoid the temptation to record your entire career history in a cover letter – all this does is undermine your careful work constructing the résumé.

Section 1: Why you are writing

Should include the reason for your letter – that is, you want to apply for a specific position. It is important to state the following details to clarify the position you are applying for. The company may have more than one vacancy being advertised and you want to make sure you are considered for the role you want. Include:

- the title of the position, including any reference numbers;
- where and when it was advertised.

Section 2: Your core career and personal experiences

This section should explain what career and personal experiences you have to do the job well. For example, you could highlight specific positions from your career that are directly relevant to the advertised position. This could also include a list of the key tasks needed to perform the role you are seeking – demonstrating that you have completed the requirements of the role very successfully, previously in your career.

Section 3: Your personal strengths

We discourage listing 'personal strengths' in a résumé because it is a factual document and there is no way to verify someone's personal strengths. However, in a cover letter, this is acceptable. Cover letters are personal letters of introduction, so highlighting personal strengths are not out of place.

Use this section to bring to the fore your strengths, personal qualities and qualifications, showing how they have benefited previous companies and explaining the value you can add to the new company.

Also outline what professional advantages you can offer the company if they employ you.

You want to ensure that the main aspects and keywords in the advertisement or position description are 'mirrored' within the cover letter. For example, if the advertisement states that they are seeking an 'honest and focused individual', you could place in the cover letter that you are a 'person with integrity, who focuses on setting and achieving business goals'.

Section 4: Your contact details

Let the potential employer know when and how they can contact you. If you can't take calls during the day, let them know that they can contact you after hours on your mobile or by leaving a message. Ensure you include all your contact numbers at the bottom of the letter.

If it is difficult to get hold of you, a potential employer may give up trying and you will miss out on the job opportunity.

Check your grammar and spelling and get trusted friends to also check it.

Remember, as with your résumé, each cover letter should be written with one job or employer in mind. Tailor both your résumé and your cover letter to the employer and the position – do not recycle old cover letters or copy directly previous résumés.

Cover letter template

Date

[space]

Contact details of the person you are writing to

Email/Postal address

Company

Dear [contact name] or [position], [if you do not know this, write Dear Sir / Madam]

I wish to apply for the position of POSITION NAME (Reference Number XXXXX), which your organisation recently advertised. Please find attached my résumé, which highlights my achievements associated to the areas of [insert relevant areas].

Currently I am employed by XXXXX as a XXXXX. Some of my key responsibilities within this role include:

- XXXXX
- XXXXX
- XXXXX

Prior to this, I have been employed within / I have enjoyed a strong career within [provide one-sentence general summary].

[For example: Prior to this, I have a strong career within business administration, finance, banking and customer services.]

I believe I have proven throughout my career that I am [use keywords from the job description or advertisement].

Or:

I believe I have demonstrated during my time with [company name].

Or:

My personal skills/strengths include [list these].
I am qualified [add qualifications relevant to the job] which I believe would provide a solid foundation for this position.

I hope to have the opportunity to discuss this exciting position further with you. Please feel free to contact me on my mobile or on my home telephone number after hours to answer further questions you may have about my application.

Yours faithfully,

[your name]

Phone:

Mobile:

Email:

Cover letter example (business)

21 October 2011

Steve Mills
Human Resources Manager
ABC Company

Dear Steve

I wish to apply for the position of Client Relationship Manager, which your business recently advertised. Please find attached my résumé, which highlights my achievements associated to the areas of key account development, project leadership and financial management.

Since 2008, I have been employed as a Business Manager/ Consultant at Business Control Systems Limited. Some of my key responsibilities in this role include:

- leading relationship management with key stakeholders and agencies;
- managing all financial services, including monthly reporting, budget setting and statutory reporting;
- supervising the operations of three retail outlets with a turnover of $8 million per annum;
- overseeing development and operation of all IT systems and administration.

Between 2001 and 2007, I was employed by Relevant Technologies in New York. Commencing as the Contracts Manager, I was promoted in 2004 to the role of Business Support Manager. Key aspects of this position included developing, implementing and managing all contracting processes, including service specification development, documentation and training.

I believe I have proven throughout my career that I have a number of key skills and attributes that meet the requirements of this role. These include:

- Excellent communication and relationship management skills, with the ability to develop trusted relationships with customers, business partners and stakeholders;
- Strong IT and MS Office literacy, as well as solid database knowledge;
- Proven written and verbal skills, with the ability to produce highly professional management reports;
- Strong time management skills, well organised and can work successfully to deadlines;
- Flexible and enthusiastic team member, with a 'can-do' attitude to all projects;
- High level of perseverance and the ability to influence and persuade.

My qualifications include a Bachelor of Business Studies (majoring in Accounting), which I believe provides a solid foundation for this role.

I look forward to discussing this exciting opportunity further with you. Please feel free to contact me on my mobile or on my home telephone number after hours to answer further questions you may have about my application.

Yours faithfully,

Joan Smith
Telephone: (09) 555 5678
Mobile: (021) 555 1234
Email: joansmith121@email.com

Cover letter example (student)

21 October 2011

Steve Mills
Human Resources Manager
ABC Company

Dear Steve

I wish to apply for the position of Helpdesk Administrator, which your organisation recently advertised. Please find attached my résumé, which highlights my qualifications in Information Systems and e-Commerce.

I am passionate about developing a strong career in the IT field. I have completed a Bachelor of Commerce & Administration (with a double major in Information Systems and e-Commerce) at the University of Cambridge in 2009. Some of the key papers I completed during this degree include:

- Information System Development
- Advanced Project Management
- Strategic Information Systems Management
- e-Commerce Principles
- Advanced Database Management & Programming
- Internet Design & Development
- Advanced Topics in e-Commerce

In addition to this, I have gained solid work experience in a number of customer services and sales roles during my studies.

I believe I have proven throughout my career that I have a number of skills and attributes which meet the requirements of this role. These include:

- genuine passion for the IT environment, with a positive approach and a 'can-do' attitude;
- desire to build my skills supporting network infrastructure, telephony platforms, production servers and client devices;
- quick to learn new principles and a strong focus towards on-going learning and personal development;
- proven ability to multitask, a high attention to detail and able to work to deadlines.

I look forward to discussing this exciting opportunity further with you. Please feel free to contact me to answer any questions you may have in regard to my application.

Yours faithfully,

John Smith
Telephone: (09) 555 5678
Mobile: (021) 555 1234
Email: johnsmith333@email.com

Enhancing your chances

With regard to your cover letter, points that will enhance your employment chances are:

Sending your cover letter addressed to a specific person. The reasons are:

1. You can ring after a few days to see whether your application was received.

2. Phoning the addressed recipient will build up a rapport with them.

3. While talking directly you may find out whether there is an interest in your application or the person you are talking to may have some questions they can ask that will speed up the process.

4. You can follow up again and see how your application is proceeding.

Very important

Recruitment consultants are more likely to do something for someone who has contacted them and built a personal connection or rapport. Most applicants do not ring recruiters. They just send a résumé. Recruitment consultants appreciate the time taken by someone who gives them a call.

If you do not know the name of the person who is taking the applications, ring the company and ask. When you speak to someone at the company make sure you ask for the correct spelling of the person's name.

Check out www.tomoneil.com/templates.html for a free MS Word cover letter template.

Section III

Interviewing basics and techniques

What are interviews all about?

Generally speaking, all questions recruiters and HR staff ask during interviews come down to two fundamental points:

- Can you do the job?
- Will you fit into the team culture?

Their job is to assess you against the key aspects of the job and company – that is, to judge your skills and abilities and make their recommendation to the employer.

They assess your future potential from your past experience. This is why it is VITAL to know your achievements and what you can offer the company (see 'Discovering your achievements', p. 14).

Dealing directly with a company, the interview process usually takes place over two to three interviews:

Interview 1: Can you do the job competently or well?

Interviews 2 & 3: Can we work with you as a person – will you fit our culture?

Being prepared is the key

To ensure you present at your best, you must BE PREPARED.

A large percentage of the time the most suitable person for the available role does not get the position.

The candidate who is best prepared will gain the role on most occasions. If you have an understanding of the prospective business – that is, you know how big or small the company is and understand their particular needs – you will appear to have more understanding in the employer's eyes and will be more likely to get the job over other candidates with greater experience who turned up for an interview unprepared.

The person that is most prepared is a person who:

- has a well-structured and tailored résumé;
- knows about the company and its products;
- has strong verbal references for the recruiter to contact;
- has good questions to ask about the role and company.

They will appear to be the best candidate (even though they may not have the best qualifications or experience), and they will get the job.

What is the interviewer seeking in an employee? The technique of 'mirroring'

Determine what employers are seeking in a candidate through evaluating job advertisements and position descriptions.

As mentioned earlier, in most job advertisements and position descriptions, there is a section entitled personal specifications/characteristics. This section is the key to the role and this is what you need to target.

Read through the documentation and summarise what the ideal person would look like. With your skills, achievements, qualifications and experiences, how can you meet or exceed these requirements?

Target the keywords and 'sell them back' to the employer

When a top, bespoke tailor makes a suit for a client, he takes measurements to ensure it will fit perfectly. Remember to tailor your whole approach to the position for which you are applying. This will significantly increase your chances of reaching the interview stage.

Accordingly, you want to ensure that the main aspects and keywords in the advertisement or position description are 'mirrored' in everything you send and in your responses at any interview.

If an advertisement states that an employer is seeking an 'honest and focused individual', you might state in an interview that you are a 'person with integrity, who focuses on setting and achieving business goals'.

Other examples include:

- Honest or possessing integrity

- Customer driven or client focused

- Proactive or keen to pursue new opportunities

- Team player or works well in a group

- Autonomous or self-directed

- Hands on or practical

Become the solution to the employer's problem.
This is what will get you the job.

Passion – the underused trump card

A very underused, but highly effective, technique to gain the job of your dreams is to demonstrate your passion and enthusiasm. Passion drives us to achieve more in all areas of our lives and calls us on to bigger and better things. As Oprah Winfrey says, 'Passion is energy. Feel the power that comes from focusing on what excites you.'

If you get to an interview, but realise that you are deficient in a key area (for example, you do not have a specific degree or the direct industry experience that the employer is seeking), it is even more important to demonstrate your passion for the role or industry.

For example, while I have a strong background across many industries, I have spent no time in the marine sector. However, if I applied for a role in that industry, I could point out the fact that I have 15 years' sailing experience, spent three years as the vice president of the Waiuku Yacht Club and own a 30-foot racing yacht. While this does not point to my direct knowledge of the sector, it demonstrates my genuine passion for the marine area and tells potential employers that this would not be 'just a job' for me.

If you can communicate this passion effectively to an employer, they may well choose you over a more qualified candidate with 10 years in the sector who showed no real interest in the position other than it will pay them a salary.

Types of interviews

If possible, try to find out what sort of interview you will be going into prior to turning up. It is harder to focus if you are expecting a one-on-one interview and then find you are being grilled by a panel of six.

The main purpose of this process is to give the interviewer(s) a chance to assess your suitability and for you to demonstrate your personality, skills and abilities.

It is rare to only have one interview prior to receiving a job offer. Most employers interview their candidates between two to four times to be sure the candidate will not only be able to do the job but will fit well into the company culture.

The STAR method

The STAR method (Situation, Task, Action, Result) is an excellent way to answer questions where the interviewer is seeking a specific example to a question they pose (see 'Behavioural interview', p. 61). For example:

'Give an example of a time you went beyond the standard requirements to assist a customer. What did you do and how did you know the customer was satisfied?'

You should answer in the following way:

Situation: Give a quick overview of the environment that you will talk about in your answer took place in. Include the company / organisation you were working for and your position. This situation is usually taken from a previous role you have worked in. However, use volunteer experience, or a relevant life event, if you do not have a suitable employment example.

Task: Outline the main issue you needed to solve and what you needed to accomplish. Remember to provide a specific incident or experience, not a generalised description.

Action: Describe in detail exactly what you did and actions you took when responding to the situation. Even if you are discussing a group project or setting, describe what you did – this is what the interviewer is seeking.

Result: Describe the positive outcome of the situation. What happened? How did the event end? What did you accomplish? What did you learn?

If you have trouble answering behavioural questions, think about it like telling a story: what happened, who was involved, and how it ended.

Face-to-face interview

This is the most common situation and takes place with a recruiter or manager interviewing you. Ensure that you listen to the interviewer well and engage them in the process. Make positive eye contact and use appropriate body language.

Attempt to establish a positive rapport with the interviewer and show them that your skills, abilities and personality will benefit the company. Do not over-reach, however, or seem too familiar.

Panel / Committee interview

In this situation, you are faced with between three to seven interviewers. This is a great opportunity to highlight your presentation and interpersonal skills in a group context.

Try to assess the individual personality types of each interviewer and meet their needs. Engage with each person at their level. Before the interview you may be told who will comprise the panel. If possible, do some research on these people through the company's website as well as a business portal like LinkedIn. But again, do not appear over-familiar.

As you answer questions during the interview, keep your main eye contact on the person who asked the question, yet spread your answer and eye contact evenly among the rest of the panel/committee members. (For example, direct 40 per cent of your eye contact on the person who asked the question and 20 per cent on each of the remaining three interviewers.)

Try to find a 'happy smiler' on the interview panel, and keep referring to them during the process. When they smile at and engage with you, you will feel better and more relaxed, and will therefore perform better.

Behavioural interview or Behavioural event interview

The Behavioural Event Interviewing (BEI) technique is when you answer an interview question giving real-life examples and facts from a specific situation. The key premise behind this type of interview is that your previous behaviour is the main predictor of your future potential. Example questions include:

- 'Describe a time when you were faced with a stressful situation that demonstrated your coping skills.'

- 'Give me a specific example of a time when you used good judgment and logic in solving a problem.'

- 'What is your typical way of dealing with conflict? Give me an example.'

- 'Tell me about a recent situation in which you had to deal with a very upset customer or co-worker.'

- 'Tell me about a time when you have gone above and beyond to satisfy a particularly difficult customer.'

The interviewer is looking for specific answers. Identify things such as names, dates, places, dollar value, etc. However, remember to not breach confidentiality with any current or previous employers.

Use the STAR method (p. 59) to answer these types of questions effectively. Or use the O'Neil Major Achievements Questionnaire outlined in the 'Discovering your achievements' (p. 14) section to pull out specific examples of personal achievements and generate specific answers to these types of questions.

Telephone interview

Telephone interviews are increasingly used by companies as a key part of the initial screening process. A large amount of the time they are assessing your language skills and how you project yourself on the telephone.

You may find it easier if you stand up when you are being interviewed on the telephone. I find when I am talking with a customer or being interviewed for a news story, I stand up as this takes me away from any distractions and helps me to better control my voice and overall demeanour.

Treat a telephone interview as professionally as you would a face-to-face one. Prepare and prepare again.

Try to find a space away from distractions, such as co-workers, children or pets.

Have a copy of your résumé in front of you so you can refer to it when required. This will also provide comfort during the process.

Focusing on the interviewer and their questions is the main priority during the interview. Use the same rules during a telephone interview as you would during a face-to-face interview (except, obviously, for eye contact and body language).

Group interviews

A group interview is when a group of people (say, four to ten) are asked to complete a task or come up with an idea together. Group interviews are designed to assess leadership potential within a body of people and the setting is usually somewhat informal.

Often there is a task to complete and the group as a whole develops a solution. Achieving a solution is not the goal of the group interview, however. The interviewers are assessing leadership potential and want to see how you relate to others in the group. Are you empathetic, friendly, a pushover, rude or aggressive?

Be friendly and agreeable in the group, yet stand by your convictions. Many people think if they steamroll over everyone else in the group, they will be seen as the key leader, not realising they are being viewed by the interviewers as an arrogant 'know-it-all' who cannot work in teams.

Lunch / Dinner interview

Be careful in these situations. Although the setting is informal, you are still being judged as you would in any normal interview setting.

Use the interview to develop a positive rapport with your interviewer and follow their lead in what they eat and drink. If you do decide to drink something alcoholic, take small sips. Getting drunk will negatively affect your overall interview performance.

Please also avoid messy foods like spaghetti bolognaise or barbecue pork ribs.

Competency / Criteria interview

These interviews are structured to reflect the competencies or attributes an employer is seeking for a particular position. These are
usually detailed within the job specification or advertisement.

Make sure you have read the job description/advertisement in
full and have a complete understanding of what the employer is
seeking.

Prepare sample questions as if *you* were preparing to interview
someone for the position. Once you have created these, collate sample
answers that you feel would meet the competency requirements.

Accurately reading the interviewer

Allison Mooney, professional speaker and author, details in her book
Pressing the Right Buttons the four key Personality Plus© types. This
is highly useful for a candidate as it will allow you to 'speed read'
the interviewer and give them the answers they need in a format
they understand. The four key personalities are:

Playful

Look for:

- Stylish dresser. Colourful and definitely eye-catching.
- Loud, talkative, relational, fun-loving.
- Smiley eyes, mixes easily, impulsive, wide body gestures, and inviting.
- Extrovert and optimistic.
- Drifts in and out of conversations according to the interest of the content.

Environment:

- Messy and lots of pictures of friends socialising.

Listen for:

- The question – 'Who?'
- Focus on relationships.

Respond to them through:

- Attention
- Approval
- Affection
- Acceptance

Powerful

Look for:

- Functional and power dresser.
- Strong presence. Decisive, fast-moving approach.
- Quick grab for control and no chit-chat.
- Direct and dominates the conversation. Has a self-confidence about them; may be restless.
- Talks about business competency.

Environment:

- Trophies and awards.
- Clutter, but they know where everything is.

Listen for:

- The questions 'What? and 'When?' They want results.

Respond to them through:

- Credit and appreciation
- Loyalty

Precise

Look for:

- Classic dresser and well-mannered.
- Thinker, organised and formal.
- Strategic approach, with organisational activity the highest priority.
- Selective listener.
- Talks about specifics and reasoning.
- Closed about their personal lives.

Environment:

- Charts / graphs, credentials.

Listen for:

- The question 'How?' or any relating to wanting more detail and facts.

Respond to them through:

- Sensitivity
- Space
- Silence and support

Peaceful

Look for:

- Comfortable clothing.
- Easy to be with. Relaxed, quiet and unflappable.
- Good listener and a calming approach.
- Sitting or leaning where possible.
- Measured with their gestures. Gentle.

Environment:

- Old relics and keepsakes on desk. Family picture.

Listen for:

- The question 'Why?' They want reasons.

Respond to them through:

- Respect
- Harmony
- Value

Great questions to ask yourself during the interview to determine the interviewer's personality type include:

- Are they loud or quiet?
- Do they move with purpose and focus?
- What questions are they asking?
- How can I weave how they see the world into the conversation?
- Whether they are loud (probably Playful or Powerful).
- Whether they are quiet (Peaceful or Precise).
- Do they move quickly? (Playful or Powerful).
- Are they calm? (Peaceful or Precise).

As Mooney writes in her book, 'Remember to treat others as they want to be treated in the interview – not how you wish to be treated.'

How to deal effectively with recruiters

Recruiters are salespeople. Some of them will treat you poorly. However, do not allow yourself to be easily offended. This is sometimes hard as many recruiters will not return your email or calls.

Understand that they do not work for you – they work for the company. They, in fact, sell a product: you. If you imagine yourself as a car, your suitability depends on whether or not you as a car meet the requirements of the purchaser (the employer).

General things to remember:

- Recruiters are the 'gatekeepers' to many jobs. You must treat a recruiter with the same respect you would an employer.

- If you miss out with a recruiter, keep applying for any new roles they may advertise as they probably have forgotten about you and what you can offer. Recruiters also keep advertising new roles to gain new candidates and improve their talent pool.

- Understand that if you met with a recruiter two weeks ago, and they now have trouble remembering who you are over the telephone, they have probably interviewed between 40 and 80 new people and have read over 200 résumés in the meantime. Therefore do not take it personally.

- Keep in contact with recruiters and be positive and friendly.

- Do not only meet with one recruiter and then expect them to find you a job. The best recruiter in the world is only as good as the vacancies they have available and their contacts. Therefore spread yourself around between recruitment consultancies to ensure you are getting good coverage and exposure to employers.

- If you want to make a complaint at some stage about poor treatment by a recruiter, wait until you have a new job then make a complaint.

Until that time, do what they ask as they hold the key to meeting with the employer.

Psychological testing / Psychometric assessments

It is highly likely these days that you will be asked to complete a skills or psychometric test at some stage of the interview process. As a candidate, it is important to be fully informed about the assessment process you may well be experiencing. Ask the employer if there will be any tests, and if so what sort of tests you will be completing. Will they be a personality assessment (what sort of person are you?) or competency / skills-based assessments (numerical / written reasoning / MS Word, etc.)?

Make sure you take a watch as some tests are done under time constraints to make them even more challenging to complete.

Numerical reasoning

In a numerical reasoning test, you answer questions using a range of facts and figures that are presented to you in a variety of ways. For example, a table, graph, series of numbers or associated tools. You are then given a range of questions and multi-choice answers based on this data.

Only one option is, of course, correct. You may want to use an extra sheet of paper and / or a calculator to work on the answer. Always ask whether a calculator is permitted in the test as you do not want to be seen as cheating.

Visit the following link for some sample numeric tests: www.shldirect.com / numerical.html

Verbal reasoning

In a verbal reasoning test, you usually complete the answers by selecting something similar to the following:

A – True

(The statement is true based on the passage of information presented.)

B – False

(The statement is not true based on the passage of information presented.)

C – Not sure

(You are not sure whether the statement is true or false as there is no information presented regarding it.)

Visit the following link for some sample verbal reasoning tests: www.shldirect.com/verbal.html

Personality questionnaires

Personality questionnaires assess your behavioural preferences in relation to your career and working style (for example, introvert/extrovert). They do not measure any specific abilities but attempt to assess how you view yourself, how you interrelate with others, how you problem-solve key issues and how you deal with difficult circumstances.

Personality questionnaires come in a wide range of formats. For example, you may have to rate yourself against a set of specific requirements. In other formats, you may have to make difficult choices between different statements.

Generally speaking, there are no wrong answers. However, an employer could want a more extroverted person for a sales role and a more detail-focused person for a data analysis role.

Personality questionnaire example questions

Examples of the kinds of questions a personality questionnaire may contain are given in the box on the next page.

Rate your response according to the following statement:

Select 1 – If you strongly disagree with the statement

Select 2 – If you disagree with the statement

Select 3 – If you are unsure

Select 4 – If you agree with the statement

Select 5 – If you strongly agree with the statement

1	I dislike meeting new people	1	2	3	4	5
2	I enjoy managing people	1	2	3	4	5
3	I am very creative	1	2	3	4	5
4	I get disappointed easily	1	2	3	4	5
5	I enjoy fixing things	1	2	3	4	5

Visit the following link for some sample personality questionnaires: www.shldirect.com/personality_questionnaire_examples.html

How can I prepare effectively for psychometric testing?

Follow all instructions given by the administrator. If you don't understand something, ask the administrator immediately. One of our favourite assessments asked candidates to first read a box of instructions on the first page, prior to starting the test. After three lines of general information, the instructions then stated 'This test is designed to ascertain how well you can read and follow instructions. If you read this, please turn the page over, sign your name and immediately leave the testing area.'

Candidates who did not read the guidelines didn't realise this assessment was effectively a trick, designed to ascertain whether a person actually read the instructions in the first place.

Any participants remaining would then go through and answer questions like 'If you were a fruit, what sort of fruit would you be and why?' It was always amusing giving this test to a roomful of candidates and watching one or two people immediately turn their test over, write their name and storm out, while the other 95 per cent waxed lyrical about being oranges, apples, bananas and the like . . .

Don't spend too much time on any one question. If you are struggling to find an answer, skip to the next one. On many occasions there will be tight time constraints, so it's vital to complete as much of the test as possible.

If you will be completing a numeracy-based assessment, ask if a calculator can be used. If not, you will need to very quickly brush up on your manual mathematics skills.

Sit a whole range of practice tests online. The more familiar you are with different types of assessments, the more you will be prepared for whatever is put in front of you on the day.

Can personality tests be faked?

Many personality tests used in recruitment contain an internal checking mechanism to assess candidates' attempts at faking the results. On most occasions these can easily be picked up by a qualified assessor.

The more important question you should ask is why would you want to fake the results of a test? If you successfully changed your answers to meet the requirements of a sales position, for example, you may end up finding yourself in a job that you are not skilled in and do not like. If you are a quiet and introverted person, you will quickly find yourself becoming stressed with having to constantly meet challenging sales targets, perform cold calling, telemarketing and persuading people to buy products from you. At the end of the day, it is in your best interests to not try to 'tweak' your results.

While tests tend not to be overly fun to do (especially under time pressure), never moan or protest about having to do them. Everyone reaching the final stages of the process will have to complete the same test, so you only single yourself out as a potential troublemaker if you start to complain.

Be professional in your record-keeping

If you are regularly applying for jobs, all your hard work may well be lost if you do not take a disciplined approach to record-keeping. It is vital to know to where and when you sent all your applications. Set up a recording system (either on paper or electronically) and make sure you include the following details:

- Job title
- Company name
- Contact person
- Date résumé sent
- Résumé confirmation (confirmation that they received the résumé)
- First interview
- Thank-you note sent
- Second interview
- Notes/general

 Check out www.tomoneil.com/templates.html for a free MS Excel job progress template.

Dressing to win

In a 2011 online poll, 82 per cent of respondents agreed with the statement 'Workplace dress codes are slipping'. In the accompanying article, a lawyer at a top-tier firm said young female lawyers wore the same outfit 'on a Monday morning at the office that you see at a club on Saturday night'.

Our dress standards may be slipping, but an interview is the key time to ensure that you are seen as a strong candidate who presents themselves professionally.

It is important to think about what you will wear to the interview three or four days in advance. Make sure everything fits, and give yourself enough time to buy a new shirt, get new shoes or dry-clean your suit if needed.

Wearing a professional outfit may not guarantee you the job, but wearing inappropriate clothes will definitely count you out. As a general rule, think about what the person interviewing you will wear as they go about their day-to-day business and dress one notch up from there. It is far better to be overdressed than underdressed. Being underdressed will destroy your confidence in an interview.

A friend of mine once relayed a story about a young man going into a sailmakers for an apprenticeship. As he was neatly dressed in a suit, he received some sniggers from the floor staff who were all dressed in shorts and teeshirts. However, the manager who employed him was also dressed in a suit and offered him the job on the spot. The young man demonstrated he took the opportunity seriously and portrayed himself as a professional who was ready and willing to learn.

If you are not sure about the company's dress code, check with the person who scheduled your interview or contact the HR department and ask. They will be genuinely pleased that you care enough to find out.

Accessories

Do not have too many distracting accessories. For example, large/ noisy bangles, gaudy necklaces or giant ear-rings just distract from your overall message and what you are trying to communicate in the interview.

Piercings

We once interviewed a candidate who had eight eyebrow rings, for the role of sales representative. We asked if he was prepared to take them out for the interview with a rather conservative client, and his response surprised me: 'I want to sympathise with the pain my wife went through when she had our children,' he said. 'Having them in my eyebrow helps me to feel the pain she went through.' Obviously he did not understand that the pain of childbirth exceeds that of getting an eyebrow pierced. He also placed his sympathy with her pain ahead of providing for her and their children financially. We did not send him to the interview and didn't put him forward for any other roles with our consultancy.

Perfume / Aftershave

Do not over-apply these products. The interviewer does not need to be able to smell you over the far side of the room.

Hairstyle

If you are going for a professional role, always have your hair looking professional and relatively conservative. Unless you are applying for a creative role in advertising or fashion, strange colours and weird looks do not work. Again, they distract from your key message of what you can offer the company.

Tattoos

Hide tattoos as well as you can. If you have them on your forearm, wear a long-sleeved shirt.

Clothing – Women

Do not wear anything low-cut or revealing. Showing large amounts of cleavage or having a high skirt is just cheapening the interview, as the candidate may be perceived to be trying to get the role through their sex appeal. If you have to resort to wearing something sexy to get the job, do you really want to work with the type of people who would employ you?

Make-up should be light and used just to enhance the natural features of your face. Do not cake on the foundation or apply bright lipstick.

If you are going for an administrative role, remember that you may need to do some PC-based testing. Therefore, fake nails should be kept to a minimum length. On one occasion we had to give a candidate a pair of scissors to cut back her brand-new fake nails so that she could complete a typing test the clients had asked for.

Clothing – Men

Please, no wacky ties (overly gaudy, animal prints, etc.). They just make you look like a joke. Also, no bow ties. The only professionals that can get away with wearing these are people who have a red nose, wear size 18 shoes and work for a circus. Never wear shorts to an interview. Shorts say, 'I am not really interested in this position.'

What not to bring to the interview

Just as important as what to wear, is what to not bring to an interview. Remember you are being judged *every second* you are being interviewed. Things not to bring (or at least put in your bag / briefcase before arriving) include:

- iPod / MP3 player
- Magazines
- Cigarettes
- Gum
- Large / bulky / unprofessional handbag
- Family member or friend hanging out in the reception area (or carpark if it is visible).

Transport

Make sure that your mode of transport is suitable for meeting your future employer. Don't turn up to an interview with Greenpeace in a car belching smoke and leaking oil. If necessary, park up the road and walk the last three minutes to the interview. It will also give you some good time to clear your head.

Shoes

Nice shoes are critical to your whole 'look'. Too many times we have interviewed professional-looking people, only to discover that their $2000 suit is matched with a pair of battered sneakers.

Mobile phones

ALWAYS turn your mobile phone off during an interview. You are making the interviewer the main priority during the time you are together. If you forget to turn off the phone and it rings, calmly apologise, turn it off and resume as if you have not skipped a beat. *Do not answer it and carry on a conversation.* Yes – this has happened to me on various occasions and every time it leads to an immediate 'no' in progressing to the next stage.

Food

Food has no place in an interview (unless you are having an interview at a café or restaurant). Remember if you eat beforehand, to check yourself in the mirror for any food spillages. Also, never ever chew gum during an interview.

Breath

Always have a few breath mints ready in your car or handbag. Interviewing a person with really bad breath is never fun for the interviewer and will dramatically reduce your chances of going through to the next stage.

Trends

It is better to invest in a classic professional suit that will last for a few years, than the latest trendy attire that will last only a season.

Body language

According to many psychologists and experts, body language can account for up to 90 per cent of the messages you send during your interview. It is important you portray confidence, and do not take an arrogant or subservient tone.

Posture

Sit up and take genuine confidence from the fact that you have been selected ahead of numerous other candidates for this interview. Sitting up also keeps you alert and on top of your game during this stressful time. Hunching over or sitting on the edge of your chair gives the impression that you are anxious and suffer from low self-esteem. Too relaxed indicates a careless attitude and an underlying arrogance that will be difficult to manage.

Hands and arms

Try not to fiddle with your hands as this can become a major distraction for the interviewer. Ideally, rest your hands on your lap or on the table. Also be aware of clicking pens. I was once reprimanded as a candidate for clicking a pen again and again during an interview.

Try not to cross your arms as this can be seen as a defensive or 'closing off' gesture, shutting the interviewer out.

Eye contact

Eye contact is very important. However, too much is unnerving and not enough portrays a lack of confidence. In some cultures, looking directly at a potential employer is a sign of disrespect. This is not true in Western cultures and you will seriously damage your chances if you are looking at the floor all the time.

When you are answering a question, hold brief eye contact for eight to 12 seconds before looking away briefly; then re-establish eye contact. When listening to a person, establish longer eye contact, but look around every so often so you do not 'stare them out'.

In panel interviews, give the person who asked you the question the most attention, shared with periodic glances to the other interviewers to ensure they feel included.

Voice

No matter how out of control you may feel, try and keep your voice calm and measured. Do not rush answers, and attempt to portray a confidence when you speak. Do not speak in a monotone, but also do not vary your pitch too much.

We remember interviewing a candidate for a customer services role who seemed really good. The interview was progressing well until he started putting on different voices and accents and became overly animated. This started to concern me somewhat and the interview was finished soon after.

How to prepare effectively for the interview

Find out about the organisation. Use resources such as the internet or your local library. Investigate questions such as:

- How many staff do they have?
- What products or services do they sell?
- What is their internal culture?
- What is the 'going rate' of this type of role in the marketplace?
- What do you actually want as a salary? (See 'Successful salary negotiation', p. 104.)

That little bit more knowledge you are armed with may be the difference between you getting the job and not getting it.

Review your ability and experience for the job, ensuring you understand all your achievements, skills and experiences, as well as being able to relate this information to the role for which you are applying.

Set three targets to communicate during the meeting. For example:

1. Strong background in sales and account management.
2. Passion for the banking and finance industry.
3. Bachelor of Commerce degree from Stanford University.

It is up to you to ensure the interviewer has as much information as they need about your skills, abilities, experience and achievements to make a decision about taking you through to the next stage – or even employing you on the spot. If you sense there is a misunderstanding about some information, ensure it is clarified before leaving.

Confirm the address and time of the interview a couple of days prior to the interview. Also ask if there is parking or whether you will you have to catch public transport.

Know the main interviewer's name. Not many things are more embarrassing than turning up at a company of 500 staff for an interview and then forgetting the name of the person you are there to see. It makes you look unprofessional and disorganised.

Prepare answers to standard, broad questions about yourself. (See 'Common employer questions and excellent answers', p. 88.) In about 95+ per cent of interviews there are some general questions asked, which you CAN prepare for.

Practise an interview with a colleague, friend or relative. Remember – practice makes perfect.

Dress appropriately for the job: if you are going for a professional sales role, wear a suit; if you are going for a baker's job, wear smart casual. Think of what the employer will be wearing, then 'go one step up' from them. If they wear a polo shirt, wear a business shirt with no tie. *You do not want to be underdressed.*

Aim to be outside the front door of the building about fifteen minutes prior to your interview. If you are early, go for a walk, clear your mind and then enter the building about five minutes before the scheduled time of your interview.

Never go in half an hour early. Doing this does not say, 'I am keen.' It says, 'My time is more valuable than yours, so hurry up and interview me.'

There is no excuse for being late. No matter what happened (flat tyre / ran out of petrol / trapped yourself in a toilet, etc.), being late says to the employer you cannot organise yourself and should not be hired!

Get in touch with each of your verbal referees to ensure you have their authorisation to use them. Remember to thank them for the time they will be spending speaking to potential employers on your behalf.

Try to take something new to the interview, such as references and examples of work. This way you have more information and you will look highly organised (even if you are not).

Pre-interview stress

If you get 'the butterflies' (that sick feeling in your stomach), do not panic. This feeling is actually a sign that adrenaline is rushing through your body. This means you quickly become more alert to your surroundings. 'Butterflies' are a good sign that you are mentally ready. As long as the butterflies do not 'take over', you will be able to give stronger answers to your potential employer.

The only time things go wrong is when we let the butterflies get the better of us and we start sweating. A great way to relax is to do some quick relaxation exercises such as taking long deep breaths.

When someone says to you 'Don't be nervous' they are being unhelpful. You are presumably going to an interview for a job you want to be successful in getting. You have something to lose and you are exposing yourself to potential rejection from the interviewer(s). Therefore, it is okay to be a little nervous. You are perfectly normal. However, do not let the butterflies take over.

Ways to relax . . .

It is vital not to show your nerves in an interview. While you may be on edge, it is important to take some time before the interview to calm down and relax as much as possible. The following are some tried and tested ways to calm your nerves just before you step in the door.

- Listen to relaxing music on your iPod.
- Arrive half an hour early and go for a walk.
- Have a hot thermos of your favourite herbal tea ready to drink before the interview.
- Meditate or pray.
- Take slow deep breaths to improve oxygen flow and slow down your heart rate.
- Phone a family member or friend and have a nice relaxed chat.
- Eat an apple or piece of fruit (not something fizzy that will give you wind).
- Read part of an inspirational magazine, book or blog.
- Do some muscle-stretching exercises.
- Brainstorm your 'bucketlist'. A bucketlist is a list of all the things you would like to see, do and achieve before you 'kick the bucket'. (See 'Long-term career planning', p. 134.)
- Mentally write a letter to a friend.

The power of visualisation

Visualising a great interview can be very powerful and significantly increase your chances of job success. Psychologist Alan Richardson wanted to understand the effects of visualisation on personal performance. In his research study, he selected a number of basketball players and initially measured their free throw percentage success. After this, he randomly assigned the athletes to one of three groups.

Group one went to the gym and practised making free throws for one hour, five days a week for a month.

Group two also met at the court at the same time, but would be taken through a guided visualisation programme for one hour. During this time they would picture in their minds picking up a basketball, preparing the free throw and making a successful shot over and over again.

Group three was the control, and they were told not to touch a basketball for one month.

The results:

Group one, who had physically practised, improved their free throw percentage by 24 per cent.

Group two, who had not made a single free throw in 30 days, actually *increased their free throw percentage by 23 per cent*. This was only 1 per cent lower than those who practised every day for one hour.

Group three stayed stable with their initial performance.

The conclusion:

When you visualise a positive outcome, such as performing excellently in an interview, your mind starts to believe it can be achieved and works towards this goal. Create in your mind the 'finished product', showing your brain what a really successful interview looks and feels like.

Before your next interview, try this technique and see how it works for you:

- Stop and think about the environment. What does the room look like? Who is there? How does the first minute of the interview go?

- From here, start visualising that the interview is going really well. How does this make you feel? What are some positive results and emotions that are coming out of the interview? What is the feedback you are receiving?

- Finally, think about how the interview ends and the great feeling you got from an interview that went really well.

During the interview

When you arrive, open the door to the reception, relax and smile. Introduce yourself to the receptionist and be very polite. People have missed out on jobs because they were rude or abrupt to the receptionist.

When you meet the person who will interview you, have a pleasant but firm handshake.

Bring two copies of your résumé to the meeting: one for you to refer to; another to give to the interviewer if they don't have enough copies to go around for all the interviewers. This just makes you look that little bit more efficient and prepared!

The interview itself

Answer each question succinctly with no 'waffle'. Speak for 30 seconds to two minutes for each answer.

Always show good manners. Always use proper English and avoid slang.

Be enthusiastic and friendly.

Ask questions about the position and the organisation. If they have answered your questions without you asking them, say in response to the question 'Do you have any questions?' 'Yes, I did, but you answered them all for me. Thank you.' (See 'Questions to ask an employer', p. 96.)

Be your authentic self – professional, yet real. You do no one any favours by pretending to be someone you are not. Even if you get the job, everyone will see that you do not match their expectations.

Try to understand the question behind the question. In the end, every question comes down to 'Why should I recruit you?' Be sure that you attempt to answer that underlying question completely.

Only about 25 per cent of our communication is oral, or what we say. Be aware that your voice inflection, the way you sit, and the way you 'hold yourself' all count towards you getting your dream role.

Display integrity at all times. We once had a young man brag to us in response to our question 'Please give an example of how you think outside of the box?' He was very forthcoming in telling us that he had helped a previous employer illegally overcome a software security program designed to stop the use of software the company had not paid for. If this had not totally turned us off the candidate, he then informed us that he also identified a security flaw in another company's website and exploited it. Not the sort of person we wanted in our team!

If, at the end of the interview, you are excited about the position, tell the interviewer(s) that you are. Make sure they are aware that you want to work for the company and that you are happy with the role as described. Too many people have missed out on positions because they were 'too professional' and gave the impression that they were not interested in the opportunity.

After the interview

Always ensure that you follow up the meeting with an appropriate thank-you email. This is another opportunity to sell yourself to the employer and will only improve your chances. An example of such an email is given in the box on the next page.

Remember to always act with integrity when you write and send the thank-you letter. I once was to be interviewed for a senior-level

---

Dear [name of person who interviewed you]

Thank you for the opportunity to meet with you yesterday afternoon for the position of [job title].

[If relevant, add two to three lines relating to specifics you may have talked about: specialist knowledge/practical experience you have that is in line with the position's requirements.]

I enjoyed discussing this role with you and would like to pursue this opportunity further.

I look forward to hearing from you in due course.

Kind regards,
[Your name]

---

human resources role and had already printed off and stamped the thank-you letter, intending to post it if I liked the job opportunity. Arriving a few minutes early for the interview, I decided to have a coffee at a nearby café and relax before my meeting. At the café, I had a brainwave when I saw a local postbox. 'Great,' I thought, 'I can post the letter now and not have to worry about doing it later.'

Sadly, I decided to follow this very unwise suggestion from myself and dropped the letter into the box. Literally five seconds passed before my mobile phone rang. Answering it, I was informed by the PA to the manager I was about to be interviewed by, that he was sick and could we please make an alternative time. I then sheepishly told her to inform her boss that he could contact me when he was on the mend. Perhaps unsurprisingly, he never called me back to reschedule. I think it may have been a little thing called 'integrity'.

Debrief yourself after the interview. You may want to ask yourself:

- What could I have done better in that interview?
- What questions have I not heard before?
- Did I answer them well?
- Is there a better way to answer the questions?
- What did I do really well?

If you have not heard from an employer within four to five business days of the interview, follow up with a phone call to find out about the status of your application. Always be pleasant and professional with this enquiry.

Common employer questions and excellent answers

Before you start. One of Europe's leading career specialists, Daniel Porot, studied candidates in job interviews and found that to be successful, you should try to make your answer last between 20 seconds and two minutes. Anything too short does not give enough information to the interviewer; anything longer just drags the interview on and starts to make you look too long-winded.

Personality

Tell me about yourself.

This question is almost always asked in a variety of ways. You need to prepare a short statement with three to four key points focused on the position you are applying for. Generally, talk only about career matters, unless you have relevant personal experience, achievements or qualifications that will promote you in a positive light. Ideally, you only want to provide a general overview/context for further discussion.

What are your strengths?

Because you have completed your research on the job as well as the company, you will be able to visualise what the employer is seeking. Phrase your answer in this context and give an example of each strength. For example:

- highly motivated
- driven to succeed
- committed to excellence
- enthusiastic team player
- strong verbal and written skills
- committed to self-development.

What are your weaknesses?

Choose an area of weakness prior to the interview. Only state one weakness and say what you are doing in order to overcome it. Overcoming a weakness is actually developing a strength. One thing to remember, however, is to try to make it sound genuine. The old answer 'I work too hard' just makes the interviewer want to dig deeper to get a more honest answer.

It is always fun when I ask this question and get in response, 'I do not have any weaknesses.' No matter how accomplished you are, that's an immediate 'fail' in the interview process.

A résumé I redesigned for a client had the following confession prior to my redrafting:

'Weaknesses: A good wine and the opposite sex.'

Would you see yourself as successful?

Always say 'yes' (no one wants to hire a 'loser'), and briefly detail some of your achievements and the goals you are currently working towards.

What is your single greatest achievement?

This is our favourite one as it almost always catches people out. Talk about your greatest achievement and have a passion about it. Suitable answers may include raising your children or exceeding challenging sales budgets. Remember, however, that this answer will strongly frame the interviewer's impression of you.

While consulting to a leading national insurer, we asked an older woman this question during an interview. She stared straight through us for a few seconds, then turned to the ceiling with her eyes seeming to cloud over. Turning to us again she said sadly, 'I have never really seen myself as an achiever.' While this broke our hearts, it also said that she had no self-confidence and would not be right for the aggressive telesales role we were interviewing for.

What motivates you?

Explain that of course money is important as it pays for your life outside of work. Then highlight how you enjoy the challenges of your career, working within an exciting team, etc. Make it seem that – 'Yes, money is important, but I come to work for more than money.'

Career related

Why did you leave your last job?

Here the interviewer wants to understand why you have left (or are looking to leave) and see if there were any issues or problems that you may have had and could bring to their company. Always be positive and do not tear apart your last organisation. No employer likes hearing a potential employee talking negatively about their last job. It will only give the signal that you may be trouble. Try to be honest, because most of the time the reason is perfectly legitimate. If you did have trouble with your previous employer, talk about how you wanted to develop your skills further, join a new industry or set a new career challenge. Smile a lot and try to be as genuine as possible.

What background do you have in this industry?

Be specific about the experiences and achievements you have had, and make them relevant to the position you are applying for. Sometimes you may not have specific experience, therefore talk about your passion for the industry if you genuinely have one. (For example, in the marine industry – 'I own a boat and am a committee member of the local yacht club.')

What kind of remuneration/salary are you seeking?

Look at 'Successful salary negotiation', p. 104.

What is your career philosophy work ethic?

Provide a short and positive statement that sums up your whole approach. For example, 'It is about getting the job done right, first time.' Once you have stated this, provide an example of how you have implemented this philosophy at work in the past. This approach provides a nice and complete statement that supplies a snapshot of your working approach.

How long would you expect to work here if we employed you?

Do not get specific. However, do not show a predilection to job hopping. An employer respects loyalty, not subservience. Make sure they understand that you respect the opportunity and will work hard for the company.

Have you ever been asked to vacate or move on from a job?

Obviously if you have not, say 'no'. If you have, be truthful and to the point but avoid saying negative things about the management or business involved.

Have you ever been disappointed in your career?

Always be positive and honest. Things do not always go our way in careers. There may have been instances where you did not get a promotion or meet a target. Be positive in the retelling but let the interviewer understand this instance was legitimately disappointing.

Team orientation

How would your team-mates describe you?

Highlight a couple of examples where you have assisted your team members and how they responded. Then draw a conclusion from this to state some of your key positive attributes. This provides a solid context, rather than just saying, 'They think I am great.'

Are you a team-orientated person?

Outline a few examples of occasions you have led and supported team players in their work or on projects you were involved in. Focus on the positive and highlight key aspects that are important in a well-performing team environment (supportive, proactive, loyal, etc.). Be aware that you must not be boastful, yet need to sell your key aspects.

What do you find difficult about working with team members?

Be positive and pleasant, but highlight that working with people who do not keep to a task, or who are arrogant in their approach, does not go well with you. However, make certain that the interviewer is left with the impression that you are a patient and supportive team member.

Business knowledge

What do you know about our business/organisation?

Always research the business beforehand. *Never* go into an interview without knowing about the firm and their core business. If you can find a particular area of personal interest or expertise, mention this at the interview. It shows you did your homework and will impress the interviewer. The exception to this rule is when you meet a recruiter who is screening for a company. Do not be concerned as everyone else who is applying for the position will not know who the company is either.

Why do you want to work for our business/organisation?

This is a vital question. They are attempting to find out your motivation for working for this business specifically. Briefly share your knowledge of their business and comment on how your skills, experience and education would fit well with their company. Talk about the development opportunities the company offers, your interest in the industry or their strong brand/presence in the marketplace. An employer wants you to be excited about their company and will always hire someone who has a passion for the firm over someone who does not show any interest. Once again, this is why you must do your preparation first. It is hard to be passionate about something you know nothing about.

Why should we employ you?

Highlight how your skills, achievements and experience match what the employer is seeking in the successful team member. Remember to read the job advertisement and/or the position description and respond specifically to those key aspects.

Why do you think you would excel at this job?

Highlight your skills, achievements and experiences in line with the personal attributes in the job advertisement and/or the position description. Give examples of how these aspects are what you are good at and what you enjoy.

What would you look for if you were hiring for this position?

Remember to use the personal attributes from the job advertisement and/or the position description, and slant it slightly towards your skills and experience (without giving the game away).

Tell us about your dream job.

Answer in generalities because anything specific will just pigeon-hole you. Talk about a job that has challenges and where you can work with a great team of people. This shows you are flexible and not looking to leave as soon as this 'miracle job' comes along.

Are you willing to relocate/travel for extended periods if required?

Make sure your wife/husband/partner/family are aligned with you before you answer this. Getting the job based on your promise to travel around the world when your wife is pregnant will only lead to major stress. If you do not have to consider someone else, explain that you enjoy the excitement of new challenges and environments and turn the answer into a real positive.

Professional development

What have you done to develop yourself personally recently?

Mention activities that are directly related to the opportunity. These activities are not just courses you have recently completed but could also include voluntary activities or sitting on local/industry committees or boards.

Where do you want to be in five years?

Respond in behavioural terms. For example, do not say 'In the role of human resources manager' to the human resources manager. Instead, respond in a way that shows you are after a challenge, but does not say 'Get out of my way – here I come.' A good example could be: 'In a position that provides a strong challenge within the human resources environment' (or whatever setting you are applying for).

Business improvement

Have you set up any systems or provided any suggestions that improved business performance?

Ensure you have a couple of great examples that you can promptly highlight, remembering to point out the positive result that came from these initiatives.

What have you learned from mistakes on the job?

Things do not always go to plan. Employers understand this and know that no one is Superman or Superwoman. Provide a real-life example that did not do too much damage to a business, and highlight the key points you learnt from the experience.

Management / Leadership

Describe your management style.

Describe a couple of occasions when you have led staff to achieve a positive result, then detail your style from these examples. Highlight how you managed each situation on a case-by-case basis and judged each situation on its merits.

What would previous managers say about you?

Talk about attributes that are true of you as a person (do not say 'my vibrant personality' if you are a real introvert). Be ready to provide some examples to back up these attributes. Good examples include proactive, loyal, friendly, caring, disciplined, focused and strong leader.

How are you in pressure/stressful situations?

Provide a couple of positive examples of how you were involved in pressure situations, how you coped (remember to be positive, yet real), and what steps you took to resolve them.

What qualities do you look for in a manager/team leader?

Be positive and talk about general traits that you would like in your ideal manager. Try not to make these too constrictive, and do not go on for too long. Positive traits include a sense of humour, fairness, trustworthiness and dependability.

Have you ever helped team members in a dispute?

Detail a positive encounter that you successfully resolved. Talk about the experience and highlight your constructive and high-level problem-solving skills. If this then led to the team members involved having an improved working relationship, mention this too.

Questions to ask an employer

Before you start. Always prepare questions to ask. Having no questions prepared sends the message that you are only interested in the money and do not care about the company or the job opportunity.

If the employer answers all your prepared questions through the interview without you getting to ask them, say in response to 'Do you have any questions?', 'Yes, I did, but you answered them all for me. Thank you.'

Do not ask questions that are clearly answered on the company's website or in any brochures/material provided by the employer in advance of the interview. This simply says that you did not prepare effectively for the interview and you are wasting the employer's time.

Understand also that you should not spend any longer than 15 to 20 minutes in an interview asking your questions. On one occasion a good friend and I were interviewing a candidate for a senior management role. Realistically, we could both see he was totally unsuitable for the position within the first five minutes of talking with him; however, we felt we would keep going with the interview to give him the benefit of the doubt. After 45 minutes we finished our questions and then asked if he had any. At that stage he pulled out a notebook and proceeded to randomly fire questions at us for about 30 minutes. A lot of the questions were not relevant to the role and it seemed that he had just looked at a few career guidance books and threw the top 40 questions together to impress us. When the onslaught finally finished, he put the notebook down and I breathed a sigh of relief that it was over. Sadly, he then pulled out another journal and proceeded to ask us further non-relevant questions for another 20 minutes. At the end we had to respectfully ask him to shut his notebook and drew the meeting to a close.

Below are some typical questions you could ask an employer. Do not ask too many questions as it may frustrate the interviewer. Just identify the most appropriate ones.

Teamwork

How big is the team I'd be working in?

Who would my co-workers be and what are their functions?

What is the manager's leadership style? How often would we interact?

What qualities/skills does the manager prize most in their team members?

Team management

How many people would I be managing?

How would you characterise the management philosophy of this organisation?

What sort of communication style works best with this team?

How much authority will I have in running the department?

What are the main challenges associated with the team?

Are there any difficult personalities on the staff?

What condition is morale in, and why?

Business strategy

What are the company's objectives for the next 12 months / 5 years?

What are the significant trends in the industry?

Do you have plans for expansion?

How do you see the future for this industry?

Competitive edge

What makes this company different from its competitors?

What are the company's strengths and weaknesses compared to its competition?

What do you think are the greatest opportunities facing the organisation in the near future?

What do you think are the biggest threats facing the organisation in the near future?

Corporate culture

What are the company's values?

What can you tell me about the culture and the environment?

What do you like about this company? What keeps you here?

What are the traits and skills of people who are the most successful within the organisation?

What does the company / team members do for fun?

Personal performance

How do you see me benefiting the company?

If I exceed the company's performance expectations, will there be additional opportunities to expand my responsibilities?

Would there be opportunities for advancement? How long might it be before I am considered for one?

How would you characterise successful employees in this department? What are their common qualities?

How will my performance be measured? By whom? How often?

Personal development

What does your company do to encourage further education?

What are the opportunities for professional training/further education?

What is the company's policy on providing seminars, workshops and training so employees can keep up their skills or acquire new ones?

How much guidance or assistance is made available to individuals in developing career goals?

Position specifics

Could you explain your organisational structure?

Please describe the duties of the job for me. Can you describe a typical day for someone in this position?

What would you consider to be the most important aspects of this job?

What are the challenges I would face in this position over the next three months?

What will be the greatest challenge in this job overall?

What responsibilities have the highest priority?

How much time should be devoted to each area of responsibility?

Which internal customers would I be interacting with most frequently? What are their typical expectations?

Could you tell me about the way the job has been performed in the past? What improvements would you like to see happen?

Why is this position vacant? / Is this a new position or am I replacing someone?

Why isn't this job being filled from within?

What were the major strengths and weaknesses of the last person who held this job?

What are some examples of the achievements of others who have been in this position?

Where have successful employees previously in this position progressed to within the company?

What types of skills do you not already have on board that you are looking to fill with a new hire?

How do you feel about creativity and individuality in this role?

Are there other job responsibilities not mentioned in the advertisement?

How often will I have to travel in this role?

Department strategy

What is the size of the division, sales volume, earnings?

What are the goals of this department?

What have been the division's goals in the last year, and did it meet them?

What have been the department's successes in the last couple of years?

What would be the goals of the department in the coming year?

What are the career paths in this department?

How is this department perceived within the organisation?

What problems or difficulties are present in the department now?

Salary / Remuneration

What is the salary range?

What are the package benefits – for example, mobile phone, car, health insurance etc?

Closing

I am very interested in pursuing this job further. What is the next step in the hiring process?

How soon do you expect to make a decision?

What are the next steps in the interview process?

Effectively negotiating your salary

Successful salary negotiation

Basic negotiation techniques

You can be highly successful in the salary negotiation process if you hold to some basic techniques of negotiation and have a clear sense of what you are seeking.

Employers *expect you* to negotiate your salary, so do not let the process be too daunting.

Find out what the position is paying

Before you start the process you must have an understanding of what the role is paying. You can do this in a number of ways:

1. The salary package may be highlighted in the advertisement or in the job description. While the original advertisement online or in the newspaper may not mention total salary, if you dig a little deeper, it may well be covered in-depth within the position description.

2. Analyse similar vacancies on the internet to see what information is available on their remuneration packages.

3. There are a large number of career calculators and databases that provide general analysis of what different types of roles are paying. A good start is a site like www.salary.com

4. Contact two or three local recruiters who specialise in your industry and ask for their thoughts on what a role like this would be worth.

If you are still not sure, think about what you are worth to an employer. What have you previously been paid? What are the benefits you are used to? Consider an amount you would be happy receiving if you were successful, then think of a figure you would grudgingly accept. That is now your bottom limit.

Remember that this bottom limit may also drop again for the 'ideal job'. Of course, for your ideal job there are many other benefits aside from money.

Sell yourself effectively

Why are you worth this amount of money? Why will you be an asset to the company? Come up with some concrete and tangible examples and include these during the interview.

It is not just about the money

Whenever you are negotiating your salary, do not forget to take a look at the other benefits, such as company car, mobile phone, retirement plans, medical insurance, holidays and associated advantages. These non-cash factors can make a very average salary package very attractive indeed.

Doing the deal

If an employer asks you, 'How much are you seeking for this position?', immediately turn the tables on them by asking, 'What range do you have in mind?' On some occasions, this will put the employer on the back foot and they will tell you what the company has in mind.

If the interviewer still does not reveal their figure, reply with a broad salary band, rather than a specific dollar value. For example, 'I'm seeking a salary of between late seventies through to mid-eighties.' If you are pressed about the difference in the range, explain that this depends on the other benefits (car, phone, amount of travel).

General tips

- Enter salary negotiations with a solid understanding of your skills, achievements and experience and what they are worth to the employer.

- Try not to be the first to bring up this subject. Make it seem that you are interested in the role, the company and career opportunities first, and money second.

- However, if as the second interview is closing, you are still not sure what the role is paying, find out. You do not want to go to two more interviews and complete a battery of psychological tests to find the salary is $20,000 less than you are seeking.

- Ask about further career development and learning opportunities. Job progression is an important aspect in making your salary decision.

- Make certain the person you are talking to actually has some negotiating power. This may not always be the case if you are dealing with a recruiter or HR manager. Generally speaking, the only person who can decide what you finally get paid is your direct manager (as it comes directly out of their budget).

- Salary negotiation is all about psychology and how far you wish to push a point. It does not matter how many books you read, it all comes down to the moment you have to actually sit and negotiate face to face with your potential employer.

- If you manage to gain $5000 more than you were expecting for your salary, that amounts to more than $16,500 (including interest) over three years. This equates to a modest car or boat or an incredible holiday overseas.

- Happiness is more important than salary. Having a shorter commute, more vacation time or good medical benefits might matter more than a few extra dollars.

Section V

Being proactive

What if it all goes wrong?
Hunting down opportunity

Job-hunting is to some degree like playing the lottery. The more tickets you buy, the increased chance you have of winning a big prize. You have to be in to win! From an employment perspective, the more résumés you have out there representing you in the marketplace, the higher the chance you have of an employer reading it, interviewing you and giving you your dream job. The more potential employers you can inform about your availability, the higher the chance of you becoming employed.

Take a disciplined and professional approach. Make yourself accountable to someone if you tend to procrastinate, like me. This could be a friend, your partner or a family member. You will find that you are far more disciplined and successful if you have someone giving you a 'prod' now and then.

One of the best pieces of advice I ever gained was from a poster I remember seeing when I was about 22 years old. The photo showed an old basketball hoop that had not seen a ball aimed at it in many years. Paint was peeling off the backboard, the wall was water-damaged and spider webs clung to the forlorn and rusty hoop. Underneath was written:

OPPORTUNITY

Then the words that changed my life . . .

You miss 100% of the shots you do not take.

Immediately, I was hit by the incredible truth of the statement. Successful people do not give up. They just keep going and going until they get the results they want. On most occasions they were not the most intelligent, the loudest or the bravest. Ninety-nine per cent of the time they were just the most persistent – pressing on when everyone else gave up.

You miss 100% of the shots you do not take.
It's a numbers game.

Job-hunting should become a 'nine to five' job too. Early on in the job-hunting process, there is a temptation to 'ease up' when the sun comes out, or go surfing when the waves are just right. However, to take full advantage of your unemployed position, you must treat job-hunting as a full-time role until you are successful in landing a job. If you do not take the process seriously early on, you will find that your financial situation can quickly unravel, and you will wish you had got 'stuck in' a lot earlier.

Tactical job-hunting versus the Shotgun approach

There are two main ways to job-hunt:

- Approaching companies or recruiters who are advertising available positions that suit your needs and skills (Tactical).
- Approaching companies that do not seem to be advertising positions that suit your needs and skills (Shotgun).

Applying online via job boards

Online career sites or job boards are great because you can often set up job alerts. You will then be automatically sent an email with positions that match your requirements.

The 'hidden career market'

The risk is that once you have gone through and applied to the relevant roles on the internet and in the newspaper, you think, 'Well that's it. There are obviously no more positions available today. I will now go to the beach.'

It is estimated that only 25 per cent of vacant jobs are advertised on the internet, in classified ads and through employment agencies. This is the most popular way to find work as it is the easiest way to access job openings and you do not have to market yourself too hard. The negative side to this is that all the other job-seekers are also using these ways to find work too, so competition is very intense.

The other 75 per cent of available jobs exist in the 'hidden job market'. These vacant positions are 'hidden' because they are filled without employers advertising them on the internet or in news-papers. However, finding these jobs requires a more proactive, focused, disciplined and strategic approach.

You can find out about these 'hidden' job openings by developing strong contacts and networks as well as contacting employers directly via the telephone, email or face to face. When you enter the hidden job market, you may also discover that you are the only candidate who is applying for the job.

Saving the employer money

When we suggest this approach to candidates, they generally say to us, 'Won't the employer be annoyed and think I am wasting their time?' On the rare occasion this may be true; however, most employers welcome this direct approach for a number of reasons:

- *Recruitment fees.* The average recruiter charges between 12 to 15 per cent of a person's salary to place the candidate. Thus, if you earn $55,000 a year, the employer will end up paying approximately $8000 on top of your salary for the privilege of hiring you. Therefore approaching them directly *immediately* saves them thousands of dollars. This becomes very important for a small-to-medium enterprise that does not have the same cash reserves as a larger employer.

- *Immediate solution.* If a person hands in their notice, the employer only has a very short period of time to find their replacement. If that person is not found quickly, it can become a major issue for the employer, with all the other members of the team having to 'pitch in' just to get by. Therefore, if you can start straight away, make that apparent to the employer as this may well be the difference between gaining the role and not.

- *Saving the employer time.* A manager is employed to do a particular job. However, when someone leaves, that employer now has to do their current role, plus spend an extra five to 15 hours a week trying to recruit the new team member. If they pick you instead, they will save themselves tens of hours of productive business time and they can be getting on with the job they are actually paid for.

- *Proactivity and passion.* By going direct to an employer, you are demonstrating the exact skills they would wish to have in an employee. As well as this, you are honouring them by effectively saying, 'I could have chosen anywhere where I wanted to work, but I chose you.' As an employer myself, it is always a nice feeling when someone thinks my company would be a great place to work.

- *No hassle.* On many occasions the employer would be happy to recruit a person who has an 8 out of 10 skill rating and who lives nearby, rather than search for a 9 out of 10 candidate who may end up living on the far side of town. If you live near the employer, make this very clear as they can then be assured you can always start on time and will not be held up by traffic jams and bad weather.

Get proactive and knock on doors (both figuratively and literally)

As mentioned, many employment statistics state that no more than 25 per cent of all vacancies are ever advertised. This leaves the field wide open for those who are prepared to do a little more than scan jobs vacant websites or read the vacancies section of newspapers.

Make a list of key companies you would like to work for and approach them directly. Or take your pick of the top firms in your field of interest and contact them.

This approach to job-hunting is called 'cold calling' and it puts candidates in the driving seat. You scan the employment market – rather than the job market – and directly approach firms you want to work for. This takes initiative and determination, but it is often worth the effort.

A young family friend decided to use this method recently, and visited a top five-star lodge to drop off her résumé. She was looking for any type of work and was just hoping to get a starting role so she could develop her hospitality skills further. Immediately the manager was impressed with her 'go to it' style and offered her a permanent position six days a week, five hours a day in housekeeping. Her new employer is now only five minutes down the road and the job lets her have a wonderful lifestyle.

Finally, do not be afraid to offend some people during this process. It is more important that you find a great job and annoy the odd person with a telephone call or email, than apply with everyone else to only the advertised jobs. What's the worst that can happen? The HR manager is not going to drive to your house and throw a brick through your window.

As you will appreciate, we suggest that you take both approaches in your job search (Tactical and Shotgun). As stated, it is all about the number of résumés you can get out into the marketplace.

The power of the 'elevator pitch'

Have a 10-second 'elevator pitch' always prepared, covering three to four key points you want to highlight to the employer. The term 'elevator pitch' was developed in the heady days of the dotcom boom in the late nineties. It was a term start-up companies came up with to communicate to a venture capitalist their business, its key offerings and financial returns in less than 30 seconds – the time it takes to get in and ride an elevator up 10 floors.

The key here is to use short and powerful statements that meet the needs of the employer. For example, if you were a customer services officer, you would want potentially to highlight the following key points:

- Genuine passion for helping people.
- Five years' experience as a customer services officer.
- Recently completed a diploma in business.

If you wanted the role of operations manager in the transport industry, the points may be:

- Twelve years' experience in freight forwarding and logistics.
- Excellent knowledge of importing and exporting regulations.
- Strong and trusted network within the domestic transport industry.

Have this elevator pitch always ready in your mind, as the next telephone call you answer may well be a recruiter wanting to pick your brain and find out if you are suitable for their available position.

The informational interview

Dick Bolles, author of the best-selling career guide *What Color Is Your Parachute?*, highlights a great way to get in the door of a company or industry you are interested in working for. This technique is called the 'informational interview'.

The informational interview is designed to gain information about a job, career path, industry or company. While it is not a job interview, you are sitting in front of a key decision-maker in the company and building strong networks that you can hopefully leverage later on.

Do your research on an internet site such as LinkedIn and find the name of a key person within the department in which you are interested. Contact them directly and say, 'I am interested in developing a career in sales [or whatever your field of interest is] and would like to meet with you to find out about your company and industry.'

Do not worry about disturbing them, as on many occasions they will feel flattered that you decided to contact them directly. In my 20 years in the recruitment and human resources industry, I only had one person ask to come in for an informational interview and of course I said 'yes'.

Important: Do not suddenly change the tone of the interview from informational to job-seeking. The second you begin trying to pitch yourself, the employer will feel misled and will quickly terminate the interview.

We once were approached by a woman having no luck returning

to the workforce after raising two children. She had gone down all the usual channels of applying for advertised jobs via job boards and newspapers, but as she had not been working for five years, kept running and losing against candidates who had recent work experience. After applying for 100+ jobs and not receiving a single interview, her spirit was broken and her self-esteem was at an all-time low.

We firstly helped her define her achievements so she could explain these to an employer in a succinct way. We then helped her understand about the 'hidden job market' and how a direct approach to employers could benefit her. Now all excited about her achievements and what she could offer a company, she then visited a range of small-to-medium-sized local employers with her résumé.

After only half a day, she had secured a formal job interview which in turn led to a job offer later that week. One of the main reasons why the company chose her was that she was family focused and that fitted in completely with their organisation's ethos.

Networking

Use your own personal and business networks to spread the word. Surprisingly, most people in your city know each other through probably only two to four degrees of separation. Therefore, ensure your networks know that you are seeking a new position.

People trust their friends, so if you are referred to an employer by a friend, you come with a higher level of trust than others who just come in off the street.

Time and time again we find people who have gained employment by just telling their friends and family that they are seeking work. On many occasions a company may have a new position that has just come up or a person that has just handed in their resignation. If people in your network know your skills and abilities, they are in a prime place to mention you to their employer or contact you to get your résumé ready for action.

Networks include:

- Facebook/LinkedIn
- Schools
- Clubs
- Church
- Toastmasters
- Rotary
- Lions
- Local employers
- Sports clubs
- Local pub.

What networks could you utilise today to spread the word?

Being professional on- and offline

In a 2010 CareerBuilder United Kingdom survey, it was found that 53 per cent of recruiters use social networking sites to research job candidates. Another 12 per cent planned to start using social networking sites for screening in the future. If you are an IT specialist or business professional, these figures jump significantly:

- Information technology – 63%
- Professional & business services – 53%.

Why do employers disregard candidates after screening online?

Job-seekers must understand that the information they post online is readily accessible to not just their friends and family, but also their potential employers. Fifty-three per cent of employers reported they discovered content on social networking sites that caused them not to employ the candidate. The main reasons for not recruiting a candidate included:

- Lying about their courses/qualifications – 38%
- Poor communication skills – 31%
- Racist/discriminatory comments – 13%
- Information about drinking or using drugs – 10%
- Provocative or unsuitable photographs or text – 9%
- Putting down previous employers, colleagues or clients – 9%
- Sharing private/confidential information – 8%.

As recruitment and HR professionals, we find it amazing what people will put online and share with the world at large. We have viewed photos of people almost nude, read racist comments and are always coming across swearing/foul language of some kind. It is vital that anyone looking to be employed does an assessment of their 'online self', taking down any 'dodgy information' that may be negatively perceived by an employer. What used to be behind closed doors is now wide out in the open.

However, the same study showed that you can increase your chances of a successful application through the correct use of online media. Fifty per cent of the employers questioned said they found content on the candidate's social networking site that caused them to think favourably about the person. Top examples include:

- Their profile lined up with their qualifications – 61%
- Demonstrated strong/solid communication skills – 41%
- Candidate came across as being well-rounded – 37%
- The profile provided a good feel for the candidate's personality and their 'fit' in the company – 28%

- Candidate appeared to be creative – 24%
- Provided a professional appearance/image – 22%
- Received awards and accolades – 15%
- Others posting good references about the person – 15%

A great example of how powerful a role social media can play in your career is provided by the case of Kyle Doyle, a 21-year-old resolutions expert for Australian telecommunications firm AAPT, recently got into trouble with his employer for taking a sick day off work. Unfortunately for him, he posted the following Facebook status update: 'I am not going to work. F#@& it I'm still trashed. SICKIE WOO.' Sadly, he forgot that his immediate boss was a friend on Facebook and therefore quickly became aware of his situation.

Further fallout from this story will occur when any new employer Googles Kyle. If he has open Facebook settings selected for his account, his online life will be visible and he will appear to be a poor candidate who is happy to lie to his employer.

Remember that it is not just your own content people can have access to. Friends on Facebook may have compromising photos or content relating to you on their site, so remember to visit these and ask your friends to remove any that may be perceived as negative. If there is a picture of you smoking on Facebook, but your résumé states you are a non-smoker, it can seriously undermine your integrity.

Do not use Twitter if you are angry or drunk. Quick comments made in a second have a habit of staying around.

Ensuring a positive digital footprint

There are ways, however, to use social media and the internet to your advantage. If you are a business professional, populate your LinkedIn profile with up-to-date information and start making positive contacts with other business professionals and groups online.

Ensure all online material is constructive and positive (both personal and professional) and that it reflects you as a 'whole' person.

Start writing blogs about your area of choice using sites such as Wordpress and Blogger. You will soon be seen as an expert in your area and most importantly Google will slowly build up a profile of you as a leader in your field.

Online profile checklist

Use the following checklist to assess your online recruitment 'footprint'.

- What websites do you have content on? (Facebook/ MySpace/Twitter/LinkedIn). What sites do you have content on that you may not have put up yourself (sites belonging to friends/family)?

- What is your profile saying about you? Many times these profiles include information about your favourite films, books and TV shows, religious and political beliefs, your studies and your interests. A good idea is to get someone else to scrutinise your profile and give you their honest feedback, no matter how hard it is to hear.

- Are there any photos that could be taken out of context if an employer viewed them? Photos with alcohol and cigarettes are generally viewed negatively by employers.

- Are you able to improve security/privacy settings so only 'friends'/people you have invited can view your information?

- Are there any negative comments or gripes you may need to delete?

- Are your tweets positive or informative in nature or do they paint a poor picture of you?

- Who are you following on Twitter/friends with on Facebook? What does this say about you?

- Do not talk about your job search online if you are still working for a company.

- Check YouTube for any video content you may unwittingly be a part of.

- Do a Google search on your name and read the first 10 or so pages. Anything negative that comes up, try to resolve immediately.

- Work on maintaining a professional profile and updating it regularly.

- Is any of your information online confidential in nature? If so, make sure it is deleted or hidden from the casual viewer.

Check your personal voicemail message and your email address

A poor email address can destroy any chance you may have with employment. Anything sexual, too personality driven, or just stupid is a liability. Classic examples we have seen from job candidates include:

- missrandom@xxx.com

- onenightstand@xxx.com

- fcukimdislexic@xxx.com

- shut-tha-far-cup@xxx.com

- justamess@xxx.com

- boididdathurtmyface@xxx.com

- depressedangel@xxx.com

- cruel2dabone@xxx.com

- lifeisanightmare@xxx.com

- dopeyman@xxx.com

If you want to have a fun address, make sure you also set up a work-only email account which you can check periodically during your job hunt.

My favourite story about the dangers of poor email addresses came from a job candidate in the United Kingdom. Applying for a range of roles in Wales, he was surprised to find his résumé was getting him nowhere. It was only when a large corporate replied to inform him that he had missed out on another job opportunity did the truth dawn on him. The company's reply stated: 'Thank you for your application. We received a large volume of very high-standard submissions and regret to inform you that you were unsuccessful on this occasion.' The email then went on to say: 'For your future reference, the chances of getting employed in Wales with the email address 'gladimnotwelsh@xxx.com' are virtually nil.'

Your mobile/home voicemail can also be poor quality. Check this to ensure it is also professional.

Do not leave voicemail messages like one I heard on a client's phone recently: 'Yo, this is Steve, you know what to do . . . [beep].' Also, if you are applying for a job in an English-speaking market, leave your standard message in English. It is really off-putting for an employer to phone a candidate and then get a voicemail they do not understand. The only time they will know when to talk is when the message beeps. By this stage they would have probably hung up.

Again, this is a major point of contact for an employer so make sure it is professional.

Damage control

How do you deal with the fact that you were fired from a former position when pitching yourself to a prospective employer? How do you explain a gap of some nature in your career trajectory? We are not perfect candidates after all.

If your total approach is not professional and there are some gaps or issues floating about in your career history, a sharp-eyed recruiter or HR manager should be able to sniff them out. However, as mentioned earlier, your role is to sell yourself and what you can offer an employer – not to give a list of reasons why the employer should not employ you.

Imagine if Ferrari created a supercar called the 'F70'. This new and exciting vehicle will revolutionise premium-level travel and will be the epitome of class and styling. Now imagine if Ferrari has the F70 crash-tested at both the Italian and German safety associations, with the Italian group responding with 3 out of 5 stars for safety and the German organisation replying with 5 out of 5 stars for safety. What would the marketing team have on the F70's brochure? They would have 'Crash-tested to German vehicle standards – 5 out of 5 stars.' They are not lying, but are being economical with the truth.

In the same way, we must accentuate our positives and try not to go too near discussion of any negative aspects of our career which may stand out.

Common issues

Gaps in your career history

A typical situation for many people is time missing in their employment history. Not many people have a perfect work history, moving from one job to another straight away. Because the role of your résumé is to sell you, you want to ensure nothing negative appears to turn the employer off you. Therefore, an option is to only detail the years employed in your résumé and not the months. For example:

Aug 2008–Current	123 Company Customer Services Consultant
Jun 2006–March 2008	ABC Company Customer Services Consultant

This highlights immediately to an employer that this person was unemployed for a period of up to five months. This will raise questions in their mind and may become an excuse not to employ them. A way to solve this is to frame the information like this:

2008–Current	123 Company Customer Services Consultant
2006–2008	ABC Company Customer Services Consultant

Employers will still wish to check these dates; however, they are now in direct contact with you and this can give you the chance to impress them with your great communication skills.

A friend of mine is a very senior executive and was struggling to find employment because he had a large gap in his résumé from his last employment. We asked him what he had been doing since then and he answered that he had done a bit of consulting, some software development and some business planning while trying to find full-time work. We then 'repaired' the missing portion of his résumé to say that he had been self-employed consulting to a range of businesses and had been instrumental in the development of a new HR software program. Suddenly employers saw him as a go-ahead individual with recent work experience. This did the trick and he was employed in a general management role three weeks later.

Took time out to raise a family?

Missing dates can also be perceived as an issue for many 'stay-at-home' mums returning to the workforce. Sadly, even in this day and age, a small amount of employers (mostly men) see raising a family as a very 'basic' activity that adds no value to the employment world. A great way to turn around this negativity is to highlight the time spent raising your children as an opportunity to develop new skills. Salary.com listed the key jobs of a mother as follows:

- Housekeeper
- Cook
- Daycare Centre Teacher
- Facilities Manager
- Computer Operator
- Driver
- Psychologist
- Janitor
- Laundry Machine Operator
- Chief Executive Officer
- Nurse
- Event Planner
- Nutritionist
- Logistics Analyst
- Interior Designer
- Book-keeper
- Administrative Assistant
- Plumber
- General Maintenance Worker
- Groundskeeper

Salary.com determined that a stay-at-home parent should be paid as much as $134,121 for their contributions. The stay-at-home parents surveyed said they logged a total of 92 hours a week performing the jobs above.

Following on from this, we once saw a résumé that had the following:

Jun 2005–Mar 2008   *Raising a family*

Key skills gained:

- High level of attention to detail
- Multitasking
- Event management
- Communication / Negotiation
- Budgeting
- Working independently
- Analytical / Problem-solving
- Working to deadlines
- Stress management

This ensured the reader understood that this period of time was actively spent sharpening her career skills, not just changing nappies . . .

> *Always remember that an employer who sees no value in this part of your career is not an employer you want to work for. Therefore, if you miss out on a job opportunity because of this reason, it is actually very positive.*

In the Appendix on p. 137 you will find a detailed 'Mum's Job Description' created by Human Resources Consultant Lisa Smith.

It has been a while since you worked

For some of us, time away from our careers could not be helped. This may result from a wide range of reasons, including sickness or death of a loved one, your own ill health, or even time taken to spend your lottery winnings. For any of these reasons, and many more, you probably do not wish to have your most recent career history in your résumé, if it finished four years ago. A way around this is to only include the time period you were employed in each of your roles.

For example, if you worked between 2002 and 2006 for 123 Company, and then were employed by ABC Company between 1999 and 2001, the first question that will go through a recruiter's mind will be 'What have you been doing for the last six years?' If the other candidates have a more complete work history, chances are the recruiter will not even interview you because they see you as not having up-to-date experience.

However, if you phrase the information in the following way, a recruiter will hopefully have enough interest to at least contact you to discuss the time period. In the best-case scenario, they will interview you if the rest of your skills and qualifications match the role.

Four years	123 Company
	Customer Services Consultant
Three years	ABC Company
	Customer Services Consultant

While this is not ideal practice, when the recruiter contacts you, you can then use your charm and communication skills to convince them that you are a viable contender for the role.

Bad / Tricky references

Sometimes things just do not go to plan. Your old manager may not have liked you, may have been jealous of you, or just not liked the school you went to. Sadly, to use them as a referee will only shoot down your chances to be gainfully employed in the future.

This actually happened to me on one occasion. A recruitment friend of mine contacted two of my more recent referees. One was excellent; however, the second was not overly positive. I was shocked at how this could happen, but had to get immediately into damage control mode. Because I had previously been the owner of a recruitment consultancy, I did not have another direct employer to act as a referee. I thought long and hard and came up with a number of alternative verbal referees including:

- Previous business clients at my recruitment consultancy.
- Other 'dotted-line' managers at the insurance company I had a positive relationship with (see below).
- People of note in the industry that I had developed relationships with.
- Respected individuals in the community (for example, justices of the peace and pastors).

This worked very well and I quickly had a number of trusted colleagues I could call upon.

Using 'dotted-line' managers (a manager who you did not report directly to, but still had a day-to-day or week-to-week working relationship with) also works very well. You can still use your most recent company while not running the risk of getting a bad reference from your old boss.

Self-employed

A common complaint from self-employed people is they have no verbal referees they can use. The last time they were employed may have been 30 years ago and their former employers will have moved on or even have passed away.

A recruiter completes verbal references because they wish to examine a wide range of issues such as your work ethic, honesty, ability to reach targets, etc. You should therefore ask a few current customers if they will provide a positive recommendation for you. Typical with many small-to-medium employers, the company/client relationship can be very close, with many clients also becoming close friends. Leverage this relationship if you can to help you to get referees who will make you stand out.

Be careful about this, though, as you may not want many of your current customers to know you are about to shut down or sell the company and find other employment.

Other people to contact who can speak about your professionalism and work ethic include your accountant and bank manager.

Remember it is not your job to shoot yourself in the foot, so talk around tricky subjects if possible. If there are difficult questions you think may come up during the interview process, have answers prepared for them in advance.

Remember – at the end of the day, you have to be honest and not lie to any potential employer. Any lies are sure to catch up with you one day.

Getting past the fear barrier

In many ways the hardest part of getting your résumé out into the marketplace is getting past the fear barrier of contacting people you do not know. However, remember that you are a *solution to the employer's problem*, therefore they have to hear about you.

In most cases you are either a 'profit opportunity' or a 'cost benefit' to a company. Thinking of yourself in these terms will increase your confidence.

Remember, if an employer receives your information and contacts you wanting to find out more, they see the value you can bring to their company and you are now in an exciting and positive position to sell yourself.

What if it all goes wrong?

Not having a job can massively affect your identity and who you see yourself as.

If asked 'Who are you?' What is your answer?

The job-hunting period can be incredibly stressful and worrying. Try to be calm about your approach and focus on getting résumés out into the marketplace.

Remember that job-hunting is a numbers game. The more résumés you have in the marketplace, the higher the chance you have of landing your dream role.

Dealing with the pain of negative self-esteem

If you are really running into major self-esteem issues, remember that you have strong values and you deserve a chance. Take active steps to:

- Stop comparing yourself to other people.
- Stop putting yourself down.
- Use affirmations to raise your self-esteem (the opposite of above).
- Mix with positive and supportive people.
- Acknowledge your positive qualities and skills.
- Involve yourself in work and activities that you love.

Areas of support and people you can turn to

Hopefully your family will be the place you can turn to for understanding. Be honest and open with how you are feeling.

Never be afraid to ask for help from anyone. Good areas of support include friends, a local church or clubs you belong to.

In his 10 million copy best-seller *What Color Is Your Parachute?*, Dick Bolles highlights the importance of having four key 'Support Staff'.

- Listener – when you are feeling down.
- Wise one – when you are puzzled about what to do next.
- Taskmaster – when you are lacking discipline.
- Cheerleader – when you want to share your successes.

However, professional services may also be required if things are really difficult.

Understand that everyone who has ever job-hunted has been plagued by doubt and self-esteem issues while doing it, no matter how successful they seem today.

Saying goodbye – how important is a good resignation letter?

Resignation letters are one of the more difficult types of letters to write. It would be easy to write: 'I QUIT – See you later.' However, most companies require a notice period to be given, and some studies have shown that many employers remember more about your performance during this period than at any other time.

A well-worded letter can help make these last few weeks comfortable, if not enjoyable for everyone; can help get you a favourable written reference; and help the employer to remember you well in the future if a verbal reference is required.

Never burn your bridges – you'll never know when you need to cross them again.

Rules for a resignation letter

- Do not make any negative statements about the business or people or offer ways for the company to 'improve' (in your opinion).

- Clearly state the date you intend to finish and make sure it is the length of time required in your employment contract. Allow extra time if you are able.

- Give a reason why you are leaving; however, you do not need to be too specific.

- Offer to be available to help after you finish. Indicate how the employer can contact you after you have gone, for those 'where did you put the blue folder' type questions.

- Let them know the positive points of your time with them. For example, 'great people', 'provided a valuable stepping stone in your career', etc.

- No matter how negative, worn out or just keen to move on you are, try to make the letter sound sincere, not sarcastic. These are people who know you and will most likely have noticed any decline in motivation and enthusiasm toward the company / your job.

- Check your spelling and grammar.

- Put the letter in a sealed envelope addressed to your manager, human resources manager or appropriate member of staff.

- Give it to them directly. Do not leave it in a 'pigeon-hole' or on their desk as it may be overlooked or fall into the wrong hands. Then when you come to leave there may be complications as no one will know anything about it.

- *Remain professional.*

Resignation letter structure

The basic structure of the letter should include four to five paragraphs. Avoid the temptation to be negative or sarcastic in the letter as all this does is undermine your professionalism and the quality work you have provided during your time with the company.

Paragraph one

This should include the reason for your letter – that you want to notify them of your intention to resign from your position and the date you would like to leave on.

To ensure that there are no misunderstandings, include your job title and write the date out in full. This is particularly important if it is a large company and your letter is addressed to the HR manager and not your direct manager.

Paragraph two

This paragraph should explain why you want to leave the company. You do not need to be too specific; however, you want to leave your manager and colleagues feeling comfortable about having you around as you work out your notice.

Examples include:

- I have been offered an opportunity that was too good to refuse and is in line with where I want to take my career long-term.

- I have decided to attend university full-time to obtain a qualification that would benefit my career long-term.

Paragraph three

In this paragraph you have to put in the feel-good factor that will help make life comfortable for everyone while you remain with the company.

This is where you let your employers know of the positive things about the company and the positive impact it has had on you and your career. Compliment your manager on things they have contributed and let them know how valuable the experience has been.

Do not go overboard and do not be insincere – it will be noticed.

Paragraph four

In this paragraph let them know that you are prepared to assist with the smooth transition to a replacement employee. Offer to help with training and let them know you are available to answer any relevant questions they may have after you have departed. (Include your mobile phone number and private email address at the bottom of the letter.)

Paragraph five

Thank them once again for everything they have done for you and wish them and the company all the best for the future.

Sign off 'Kind regards' with your name and contact details.

Check out www.tomoneil.com / templates.html for a free MS Word resignation letter template.

Long-term career planning

Unfortunately, most people think goal setting and career planning is something only people who own Ferraris do. Sadly, the vast majority of people spend far more time planning their wedding or buying a second-hand car than they do planning their life and their career.

As motivational speaker John Eric Jacobsen states:

'Your goals are your blueprints for the future. Goals are dreams about to be born. Goals are the ladders we climb to reach our vision of success. If you don't have goals, you end up working for someone who does have goals.'

This is why less than one in 30 people invests in motivational books and programmes and actively plans their life through formal goal setting. On a positive note, you are probably one of these people as you are reading these words right now.

When it all goes wrong

As a recruiter, it has always made me so sad to see someone like a 45-year-old accountant with two children in exclusive schools, a house in the nicest part of town and two European cars hate what their life has become. The typical story was that one of their parents had been an accountant and it seemed a safe bet for a successful career.

What their parents did not factor in when encouraging them to follow in their footsteps was that they hated finance, money and numbers, and actually wanted to be an architect. Twenty years later they now wish to change their career, but can't afford to drop $150,000 in their salary to go back to study. They are now trapped in a job they cannot stand and living a lifestyle that can only be paid for by staying in their current career. They are caught in the 'revolving door of affluence' and have become 'rat race refugees' as my good friend and professional speaker Rachel Prosser aptly describes it.

Sadly, they think because they cannot escape from their career, they only need a better-paying position at a better company to balance their life and family out. This almost never works and the person is trapped in an even more senior role that demands more time at the office, more time on the road and less time at the place that matters most – home.

Plan your career

It is vital you have a clear idea of what both your short- and long-term career goals are. If you clearly understand your long-term goals, your short-term choices and decisions will be easier to make.

Questions you want to ask yourself include:

- Where do I ultimately want to be in my life, both professionally and personally? Is climbing the corporate ladder important to me, or am I happy with a less stressful (and less well-paid) job?

- What are my strengths and what do I do well?

- To answer this, ask 10 family members and friends to give you honest feedback.

- What are my weaknesses and what sort of things do I struggle with? Again, ask your family and friends for their honest thoughts.

- What would be a great career choice to make now if I could walk into any role?

- What role do I want to be sitting in within the next 10 years?

- What role do I want to be sitting in within the next 20 years?

- What are 100 things I want to do / have / achieve before I 'kick the bucket'? [i.e. your bucketlist, p. 83]?

- What further training or qualifications do I need to attain?

- Can I do these part-time while I am employed?

- What are three things I can do this week to start to achieve both my short- and long-term goals?

- What is my next step?

Final thoughts

The job-hunting process can be crushingly hard sometimes. But our team is always there to lend a hand. Visit us at the following addresses:

New Zealand	www.cv.co.nz
Australia	www.resumeone.com.au
UK, USA and rest of the world	www.resumementor.com
Goal coaching and professional speaking	www.tomoneil.com

Appendix

Lisa Smith is a professional HR practitioner and manager at CV.CO.NZ. She created this excellent document which opens many eyes to the hard work mothers put into their day.

Job Description

HOME EXECUTIVE (Both working and non-working)

Position summary

This role is responsible for:

- Running and managing the day-to-day operations of the enterprise.

- Ensuring the financial viability of the enterprise.

- Overseeing the physical, mental and emotional development and needs of the younger (and therefore immature and demanding) team members.

- Perfectly supporting and coordinating the physical, emotional and environmental needs of the older colleagues in the team.

General responsibilities

- Manage physical needs including feeding, toileting, bathing and ensure appropriate exercise and developmental activities for younger team members.

- Primarily responsible for all aspects of health and safety.

- Maintain stimulation necessary for age-appropriate developmental activities. Offer activities and opportunities for creative play and ensure certain milestones are achieved, taking every opportunity for teaching basic numerical and linguistic, as well as social and behavioural, skills.

- Manage the enterprise's emotional (both individual and corporate) needs and requirements. Balance team members' desire for independence and space with reassurance and support. An underlying understanding for the need of discipline and character building is pivotal for this role.

- Be proactive in making and keeping health appointments, social engagements, developmental activities (playgroup and, later, kindy and swimming, etc.) for the younger team members.

- In keeping with social traditions, ensure younger team members are always dressed well and appropriately for the occasion and weather.

- Act as key decision-maker for scheduling, clothing, diet and interior décor.

- Ensure all needs are met immediately if not in advance and doing so with loving support and perfect composure in times of stress and frustration. Perfect wisdom in terms of appropriate responses to every situation is a must.

Day-to-day duties include

- Maintain a clean, healthy, attractive, stimulating and warm environment to a high standard.

- Prepare as many as six meals a day as well as snacks.

- Ensure laundry is cleaned, dried (even in the rain), folded and put away.

- Maintain a clean kitchen (including dishes, microwave, fridge and cabinetry).

- Maintain clean and organised living areas (including dusting, cleaning floors, and general tidying); outside areas to be kept tidy, even after rain, snow and hail.

- Attractive outdoor additions such as trees and vegetable gardens to be developed as well as maintained with water and weeding.

- Driving younger team members to various outside activities including doctor's appointments, shopping, friends, etc.

- Maintain personal emotional and physical health.

- Be attractive and interesting at all times for your partner.

Qualifications

- At least diploma level qualified in psychology, finance, English, mathematics, geography, logistics, beauty, education, hospitality, mechanical engineering, nursing and IT. (Bachelor's level qualifications preferred. Trade certificate in hairdressing is useful for the first three years of each team member's existence.)

Pay

- Between the ages of 10 and 18 you pay them.

- When you die, you give them whatever is left.

Benefits

- Hopefully almost unlimited opportunities for personal growth and free cuddles for life.

Online resources

Feel free to suggest other useful sites we can include in this section. Please email us at editor@tomoneil.com with your comments. If we publish your revisions in an updated version, we will include your name in our 'Professional contributors' section. This will allow you to reference yourself in any promotional material as an associate contributor to *Selling Yourself to Employers*.

General job-hunting tips and support

www.jobhuntersbible.com/

> Great tips and career hints by Dick Bolles, author of *What Color Is Your Parachute?*, the world's best-selling career guide.

jobsearch.about.com

> Lots of information giving interview tips and suggestions; résumés, interview attire, and thank-you letters.

www.quintcareers.com/

> US-based site with some excellent articles and helpful tips.

www.emc.com/collateral/article/100-job-search-tips.pdf

> Great e-book with excellent tips from Fortune 500 recruiters.

www.indeed.com

> Indeed.com searches job sites, newspapers and company career pages for employment advertisements.

Résumé development consultants

www.cv.co.nz
> Résumé development and career consultancy business owned by author Tom O'Neil.

www.résuméone.com.au
> A résumé development and career consultancy business owned by authors Gaynor and Tom O'Neil.

www.résumémentors.com
> The international résumé development portal for Tom and Gaynor O'Neil.

www.tomoneil.com
> A professional speaking website focusing on goal setting and personal development for both corporates and individuals.

Psychometric assessment

Example tests and sites:

www.shldirect.com/numerical.html

www.shldirect.com/verbal.html

www.shldirect.com/personality_questionnaire_examples.html

www.shl.com/TryATest/default.aspx

> SHL Group Limited are international leaders in testing and assessment, and have many large corporations as clients all around the world.

www.practicetests.co.uk
> Practicetests.co.uk is a great site to get quality information on

the history of testing as well as solid practical experience using a wide range of assessments.

Other pages

www.jibberjobber.com

A great tool to organise your job hunt all in one place.

www.linkedin.com

Professional networking portal and brilliant for developing key relationships as well as finding out who you need to contact for informational interviews.

www.twitjobsearch.com

This site searches positions that are advertised through Twitter.

www.youtube.com

YouTube has thousands of job-search, interview and career-specific videos all at your fingertips.

About the authors

Tom O'Neil – Bachelor of Social Science (major in Psychology)

Tom is a key contributor on interview preparation and career achievement to numerous international career guides and is a professional speaker on the subjects of personal development and goal achievement. He has been quoted in *What Color is Your Parachute?* every year since 2008. He has been interviewed on many occasions for various international television and radio shows and has had numerous articles relating to interviewing, goal setting and career development printed in a wide range of magazines and newspapers.

After founding and selling two recruitment consultancies, Tom consulted independently in human resources to a number of leading national and international organisations. After two short periods doing community support work through his church in the Philippines and India, he joined Deloitte as a management consultant specialising in human resources.

Tom now owns a number of international career development and professional speaking companies including:

www.tomoneil.com

www.resumementor.com

www.resumeone.com.au

www.cv.co.nz.

You can contact Tom direct at:

tom@cv.co.nz

twitter.com/tomoneil_com

nz.linkedin.com/in/tomoneil1

Gaynor O'Neil - Member of the Recruitment and Consulting Services Association

Gaynor is a pioneer within the modern world of recruitment and human resources. She has successfully established and sold several recruitment and HR consultancies and has written books on career matters, one of them sponsored by a leading banking group. Gaynor is the Managing Director of www.resumeone.com.au.

As well as having been employed as a weekly columnist for a national newspaper writing on vocational opportunities, Gaynor has worked with Tom in their international résumé-writing businesses.

Described as 'an icon within the recruitment industry' by a leading employment journalist, Gaynor is pleased to share her knowledge with you.

Admitted to the Institute of Personnel Consultants in 1981, she is a Certified Recruitment Consultant.

You can contact Gaynor direct at:

gaynor@resumeone.com.au

nz.linkedin.com/pub/gaynor-o-neil/10/879/b9

If you think we have omitted information, or you would like to suggest new material for addition to this job-hunting guide, please email us at editor@tomoneil.com with your comments.